Being A Dad
According To The Bible

Written and illustrated by Jeff Todd

Being A Dad According To The Bible

Published by:
Jeff Todd
Newnan, Georgia

ISBN-13: 979-8-3304-9497-2

The purpose of this book is to share God's Word that relates to the roles of men in parenting. It is part of the outreach ministry of Jeff Todd.

Please note that there will be mistakes and misprints in this book. We are all human, right? We hope you won't find too many of them. This book was edited to the best of the author's ability and he will not be held responsible for errors.

Direct all correspondence to:

A BackPew Review
c/o Jeff Todd
PO Box 71972
Newnan, GA 30271-1972

Children Learn What They Live

If a child lives with criticism,
he learns to condemn.
If a child lives with hostility,
he learns to fight.
If a child lives with ridicule,
he learns to be shy.

If a child lives with shame,
he learns to feel guilty.
If a child lives with tolerance,
he learns to be patient.
If a child lives with encouragement,
he learns confidence.

If a child lives with praise,
he learns to appreciate.
If a child lives with fairness,
he learns justice.
If a child lives with security,
he learns to have faith.
If a child lives with approval,
he learns to like himself.

If a child lives with acceptance and friendship,
he learns to find love in the world.

Author Unknown

Acknowledgements

I would like to thank my Mom:

- *for being the role model in my life*
- *for stepping up to the plate by being both a Mom and a Dad to me*
- *for helping me to grow to become a man*
- *and for always being there for me.*

And most importantly... to God... for putting the right people in my life to make me the Dad I am today.

Introduction

To be honest, I did a lot of thinking before attempting to write a guide on how to be a Dad. In my mind, I figured this was something only done by fellas with PhD's or that have talk shows on cable TV. I felt that this wasn't something an ordinary fella like me should be doing. This was out of my league.

Even though I have been a Dad since 1990, I know that I have made a lot of mistakes through the years. I'll be the first one to tell anyone that I'm not perfect. When it comes to parenting, I'm just fortunate that my kids made it out alive. But, the fact still remains... I am a Dad and my kids turned out fine. So, maybe I did do some things right.

The Lord has truly blessed me. What more can I say? I have biologically contributed to having both a son and a daughter. My son was born first and my daughter popped out next. They are spaced two years apart which allowed me enough time to slowly get my feet wet in the Daddy Game. That's pretty cool! And twenty years later, He's given me another opportunity to try it all over again by allowing me to foster two kids – two girls currently aged twelve and fourteen.

At my age, either God has a great sense of humor by giving me another chance of doing it right this time or maybe He thinks that these two will actually benefit from being in my care. It could be the simple fact that I now know He has already written a 'how-to-guide' for Dads like me to read and follow in the Bible. And this time He expects me to actually read it this go around.

Parenting isn't easy. I know this from experience. Some times it can be kinda rough and even scary. It can also be stressful and every day you wonder if you're doing a good job. You never really know for sure.

If you have children, then you know how they can mash your buttons. They can make you angry. Don't get me wrong. Those bundles of joy are cute in the very beginning and bring tons of happiness. From the moment they pop out, they are amazing little creatures; those little hands and feet and beautiful faces. But, as they grow older, they start having minds of their own. They're constantly getting into stuff and it seems like we are mostly correcting them.

"Stop!"

"Don't do that!"

"Get away from there!"

It's a never ending story, but it's not all bad. There are times when they do something cool. That's when we get to change our vocal tones to something more positive.

"Wow! That's awesome! Great job!"

"You did good! Give Daddy a high-five!"

"I'm so proud of you."

But, that's pretty much it in a nutshell. As Dads, we are leading and directing our kids by teaching them what is right and wrong. The times we tell them to 'stop' is usually for their own good to protect them. We are like sculptors with the ability to mold something great out of our children. They watch and learn from our lives, so we have to make sure we represent a good role model to them, too. Our job is very important.

So... why *Being The Dad That God Wants You To Be*? Well, I am writing this with the intentions of helping someone out there. It's not that I have a certificate on my wall for being anything special other than a simple man that cares about humanity. I do have the ability to read and I also own a copy of the Bible that provides me with all of the information I need for living. It's just a matter of opening it up.

I also know that, as a Dad, I am creating a generation of future Dads that will need my help in being the best Dad that they can be. They can learn from my mistakes and use this information I received from the Bible as a guideline. As a leader of my family, I owe it to them.

Folks, here's another serious issue. There are many kids out there in the world that need Dads in their life. There are also Dads out there that are running from their responsibilities to their children. It's time it all stops.

If this guide can help at least one person, then it's worth it. If we can change the life and direction of one person, then that's awesome. That's the purpose of this guide today. I'm willing to put the time and effort into it, but I can't do it alone.

I pray that God will show me the words to say to you and give me the messages for you to read. He will have to convict the hearts of those reading this for something to change.

Give me a minute. I would like to pray:

"Dear, Lord. I pray today that you use these words in this book to reach others. Your Word is powerful and has the ability to tear down walls in our hearts. It can open our spiritual eyes to truth. Guide us, Lord, in the path you have already set for us as the men you have called us to be. Use me, Lord, and this book to make us become better Dads and to be a light to others so that they can join us by following You. Thank you. Amen."

Well, I am feel better about this. How about you? You ready to get this started?

This is my attempt to help us all become better Dads from a simple-minded point of view...

Enjoy!

Statistics - The Boring Stuff

I like looking at statistics. It's a cool scientific way of gathering data and analyzing it. You can learn a lot from all those compiled numbers.

An example would be in baseball. Some smart person took the time and done some sort of analytical study on all of the players of any given team. The data received can tell us how good they are. If a batter comes up to the plate with a career RBI (runs batted in) of 2,000, then chances are, this fella is about to pop that baseball straight out of the park.

Statistics can be used in other areas of life. For example, a great way to understand how important Dads are to the family structure is to do a search on the Internet for statistics concerning 'fatherless children'. Now, I can't guarantee the accuracy of these claims, but we can use this info as a tool. From what I've found, you can see that there is a problem in society today.

Here's what I found from doing my own search:
- 63% of youth suicides are from fatherless homes (US Dept. Of Health/Census) – 5 times the average.
- 90% of all homeless and runaway children are from

fatherless homes – 32 times the average.
  - 85% of all children who show behavior disorders come from fatherless homes – 20 times the average. (Center for Disease Control)
  - 80% of rapists with anger problems come from fatherless homes – 14 times the average. (Justice & Behavior, Vol 14, p. 403-26)
  - 71% of all high school dropouts come from fatherless homes – 9 times the average. (National Principals Association Report)

Father Factor in Education - Fatherless children are twice as likely to drop out of school.

  - Children with Fathers who are involved are 40% less likely to repeat a grade in school.
  - Children with Fathers who are involved are 70% less likely to drop out of school.
  - Children with Fathers who are involved are more likely to get A's in school.
  - Children with Fathers who are involved are more likely to enjoy school and engage in extracurricular activities.

Father Factor in Drug and Alcohol Abuse - Researchers at Columbia University found that children living in two-parent household with a poor relationship with their father are 68% more likely to smoke, drink, or use drugs compared to all teens in two-parent households. Teens in single mother households are at a 30% higher risk than those in two-parent households.

  - 75% of all adolescent patients in chemical abuse centers come from fatherless homes – 10 times the average.
  - 70% of youths in state-operated institutions come from

fatherless homes – 9 times the average. (U.S. Dept. of Justice, Sept. 1988)
- 85% of all youths in prison come from fatherless homes – 20 times the average. (Fulton Co. Georgia, Texas Dept. of Correction)

Father Factor in Incarceration – Even after controlling for income, youths in father-absent households still had significantly higher odds of incarceration than those in mother-father families. Youths who never had a father in the household experienced the highest odds. A 2002 Department of Justice survey of 7,000 inmates revealed that 39% of jail inmates lived in mother-only households. Approximately forty-six percent of jail inmates in 2002 had a previously incarcerated family member. One-fifth experienced a father in prison or jail.

Father Factor in Crime - A study of 109 juvenile offenders indicated that family structure significantly predicts delinquency. Adolescents, particularly boys, in single-parent families were at higher risk of status, property and person delinquencies. Moreover, students attending schools with a high proportion of children of single parents are also at risk. A study of 13,986 women in prison showed that more than half grew up without their father. Forty-two percent grew up in a single-mother household and sixteen percent lived with neither parent.

Father Factor in Child Abuse – Compared to living with both parents, living in a single-parent home doubles the risk that a child will suffer physical, emotional, or educational neglect. The overall rate of child abuse and neglect in single-parent households is 27.3 children per 1,000, whereas the rate of overall maltreatment in two-parent households is 15.5 per 1,000.

Daughters of single parents without a Father involved are 53%

more likely to marry as teenagers, 711% more likely to have children as teenagers, 164% more likely to have a premarital birth and 92% more likely to get divorced themselves.

Adolescent girls raised in a 2 parent home with involved Fathers are significantly less likely to be sexually active than girls raised without involved Fathers.

- 43% of US children live without their father [US Department of Census]
- 90% of homeless and runaway children are from fatherless homes. [US D.H.H.S., Bureau of the Census]
- 80% of rapists motivated with displaced anger come from fatherless homes. [Criminal Justice & Behavior, Vol 14, pp. 403-26, 1978]
- 71% of pregnant teenagers lack a father. [U.S. Department of Health and Human Services press release, Friday, March 26, 1999]
- 63% of youth suicides are from fatherless homes. [US D.H.H.S., Bureau of the Census]
- 85% of children who exhibit behavioral disorders come from fatherless homes. [Center for Disease Control]
- 90% of adolescent repeat arsonists live with only their mother. [Wray Herbert, "Dousing the Kindlers," Psychology Today, January, 1985, p. 28]
- 71% of high school dropouts come from fatherless homes. [National Principals Association Report on the State of High Schools]
- 75% of adolescent patients in chemical abuse centers come from fatherless homes. [Rainbows f for all God's Children]
- 70% of juveniles in state operated institutions have no father. [US Department of Justice, Special Report, Sept.

1988]
- 85% of youths in prisons grew up in a fatherless home. [Fulton County Georgia jail populations, Texas Department of Corrections, 1992]
- Fatherless boys and girls are: twice as likely to drop out of high school; twice as likely to end up in jail; four times more likely to need help for emotional or behavioral problems. [US D.H.H.S. news release, March 26, 1999]

Census Fatherhood Statistics

- 64.3 million: Estimated number of fathers across the nation
- 26.5 million: Number of fathers who are part of married-couple families with their own children under the age of 18.

Among these fathers -

- 22 percent are raising three or more of their own children under 18 years old (among married-couple family households only).
- 2 percent live in the home of a relative or a non-relative.
- 2.5 million: Number of single fathers, up from 400,000 in 1970. Currently, among single parents living with their children, 18 percent are men.

Among these fathers -

- 8 percent are raising three or more of their own children under 18 years old.
- 42 percent are divorced, 38 percent have never married, 16 percent are separated and 4 percent are widowed. (The percentages of those divorced and never married are not significantly different from one another.)
- 16 percent live in the home of a relative or a non-relative.

- 27 percent have an annual family income of $50,000 or more.
- 85 percent: Among the 30.2 million fathers living with children younger than 18, the percentage who lived with their biological children only.
- 11 percent lived with step-children
- 4 percent with adopted children
- < 1 percent with foster children

Recent policies encourage the development of programs designed to improve the economic status of low-income nonresident fathers and the financial and emotional support provided to their children. This brief provides ten key lessons from several important early responsible fatherhood initiatives that were developed and implemented during the 1990s and early 2000s. Formal evaluations of these earlier fatherhood efforts have been completed making this an opportune time to step back and assess what has been learned and how to build on the early programs' successes and challenges. While the following statistics are formidable, the Responsible Fatherhood research literature generally supports the claim that a loving and nurturing father improves outcomes for children, families and communities.

- Children with involved, loving fathers are significantly more likely to do well in school, have healthy self-esteem, exhibit empathy and pro-social behavior, and avoid high-risk behaviors such as drug use, truancy, and criminal activity compared to children who have uninvolved fathers.
- Studies on parent-child relationships and child well-being show that father love is an important factor in predicting the social, emotional, and cognitive development and functioning of children and young adults.

- 24 million children (34 percent) live absent their biological father.
- Nearly 20 million children (27 percent) live in single-parent homes.
- 43 percent of first marriages dissolve within fifteen years; about 60 percent of divorcing couples have children; and approximately one million children each year experience the divorce of their parents.
- Fathers who live with their children are more likely to have a close, enduring relationship with their children than those who do not.
- Compared to children born within marriage, children born to cohabiting parents are three times as likely to experience father absence, and children born to unmarried, non-cohabiting parents are four times as likely to live in a father-absent home.
- About 40 percent of children in father-absent homes have not seen their father at all during the past year; 26 percent of absent fathers live in a different state than their children; and 50 percent of children living absent their father have never set foot in their father's home.
- Children who live absent their biological fathers are, on average, at least two to three times more likely to be poor, to use drugs, to experience educational, health, emotional and behavioral problems, to be victims of child abuse, and to engage in criminal behavior than their peers who live with their married, biological (or adoptive) parents.
- From 1995 to 2000, the proportion of children living in single-parent homes slightly declined, while the proportion of children living with two married parents remained stable.

Yeah, I know. That was a lot of boring information, but without it, we may not realize how huge the 'fatherless' problem really is. We may not even know that being a child without a Dad could

create such a dramatic situation. I mean, we see kids every day and probably don't even consider their family life. We may see them as a bunch of rebellious punks that stay in trouble all the time. But, what if the root of the problem is that they need a father-figure in their life? We could probably come up with a solution to get them back on track. What if we could change the statistics? That would be cool.

What is a Dad?

What is a Dad? Ya know, that seems like an easy question to answer. Our response would probably be something like, "A Dad is the male-figure in a family that helped the female-figure biologically produce the little offspring that has the characteristics of both of them. The Dad would be the one with the facial hair." That was a pretty simple answer. But, was it the correct one? Well, yeah... almost.

Any time you want to know the true meaning of a word, it's best to use a dictionary. In my day, this was a thick book with pages in it. Now, you can find one on the Internet. Either way, Mister Webster always seems to know the right things to say when you want to know what a word means.

I looked the word 'Dad' up and it tells me that a Dad is basically 'an informal word for Father'. So, I looked up the word 'Father' and it says that it's simply 'a male parent'. So, we were pretty close.

As I dug deeper into it's true meaning, I found that any man that offers paternal care to a child can be called a Dad. Any man? According to the dictionary, this can include:

Stepdads
Adoptive Dads
Foster Dads
Father-Inlaws
Neighbors
And even men that step up
to the plate to be a mentor
to a child

Basically, 'being a Dad' could be a title given to any male figure that is willing to take on the role of helping a child that could use the help. That's pretty cool!

Even though a man doesn't have a biological child that he helped produce, it doesn't disqualify him from being called a Dad. He could mentor a child or adopt one. Or just because our own biological kids are grown and may not need us anymore, it doesn't mean we couldn't help other children by becoming a foster Dad to them. It seems there's always job security in being a male parent. The key for us would be to plug in where we are needed.

There's always a need for parents. My wife and I drove by our local DFACS (Department of Family and Children Services) office the other day and saw a sign posted on their lawn that read, "Foster Parents Needed

– Apply Within". This is the first time I had ever seen something like this. An advertising sign at DFACS? Really? It must be a real desperate situation when DFACS has to post a yard sign to get our attention. There must really be a demand for parents out there... for both Moms and Dads. We should all do what we can to help.

I must admit. I never really put much thought into what the true meaning of being a Dad was. Yeah, I produced two of the finest specimens a man could ever produce when my kids were born. As soon as they arrived, I thought I had become a Dad. This automatically made me certified and official. I didn't need a piece of paper framed on my wall because I had living proof that I was one. I thought:

"Being a Dad is simple. I could do this all day. Make babies and watch them pop out. No problem."

But when I thought back on my own childhood, I knew I grew up as a child without a Dad. I mean, I had a biological one that made me, but he bailed out and left my mother with the role of being both parents. I knew how I felt about him for doing it, so I knew it took more than just 'making a child' to be considered one. A Dad must have some kind of responsibility where he actually has to do something.

As I think back on my Mom and all that she has done in raising me, I realize that she did an awesome job. I'm sure she can think of things that she wished she had done better, but in my eyes, she is the best Mom anyone could ever ask for. I have always given her credit for being the 'Mom' and 'Dad' in my life.

I can remember her always working every day and coming home to cook, clean and to make sure I was doing what I was supposed to. It was a daily routine and she never complained. If there's one thing I learned from her is that she has always been there for me. This is another trait of what it takes to be a Dad. We have to be there for our kids daily.

I also remember there being male figures that came into my life to help. It wasn't because my Mom asked for their help. It was more like they just appeared out of nowhere to help guide me. I never really put that much thought into why they were there. I just knew that they were tolerated as long as they didn't expect me to call them

'Dad' or buy them a greeting card on Father's Day.

Let me tell you something. As a child, when you realize that your biological Dad will no longer be in the picture, you develop a brick wall around your heart that no one can enter. Regardless of who your Mom marries or what man steps into your life, they will never replace that void. This 'brick wall' is a hard one to break. This could explain why many Stepdads have such a hard time bonding with their new stepkids. They may try to become their friend with the hopes of winning their affection, but it's a tiring situation. It will take someone with understanding and patience to build that trust that the man before them had broken. Another trait of a Dad would be a man that's willing to step up and never give up.

For this bonding relationship to work, the child will also have to realize that a Dad isn't necessarily the man that put them here. It can be the man that's willing to step up and help them get to where they are going in life. This child will have to understand that any man that steps into their 'personal bubble' shouldn't be considered a threat. Most men know that they can never really

replace a child's 'biological' Dad, but if they are willing to help and put forth an effort, maybe it would be worth giving them a chance.

It would be great if life was perfect. But, it's not. When it comes to family life, wouldn't it be cool if everything flowed like butter on hot pancakes? God has a perfect plan for humanity – He designed it, He created it and He will help us manage it if we would let Him. But, Satan does his little number in the lives of men and messes everything up for all of us. People suffer – both grown-ups and kids.

You know, the perfect scenario in a family life would be that a biological Dad would take his role seriously and be the parent that his child desperately needs. This is by God's design and the original plan that He made for the both of them. But, because man likes to change God's plans, God has to make adjustments to protect the child. The Bible tells us:

A father of the fatherless, and a judge of the widows, is God in his holy habitation. - Psalms 68: 5

God is a father to the fatherless? How is this even possible? You can't see God. How in the world is He able to do 'Dad things' with us like throw a baseball or take us camping? It means that, just because a child doesn't have his biological Dad by his side, it doesn't mean he will have to walk through life all alone because God will supply the men-figures in his life.

The problem a 'fatherless' child may have is that he may not realize God's provision. This child will have to recognize that God put those men there in his life. If not, the child may suffer the damages of having a blinded heart to what God has done.

Having the understanding darkened, being alienated from the life of God through the ignorance that is in them, because of the blindness of their heart. - Ephesians 4: 18

If a child doesn't know that God is by their side through the work of the men He has called to help, the child will feel like they are all alone. This is probably why many are led on the wrong paths to become part of the negative statistics for fatherless children.

This was a problem I had growing up. I didn't see God's provision. I had learned to accept the fact that my biological Dad wasn't there. It hurt, and like most injuries, you deal with it and it leaves a scar. For me, I kept going and buried this feeling deep inside my heart. It comes with consequences. Sadly, many kids are doing this today.

Here's a poem I wrote a few years ago that many fatherless children can relate:

The Scar
(The Cry of a Fatherless Child)

*You left no direction, you left me to be
I am who I am because of me
The joke I looked up to in a little boy's eyes
That couldn't be found to hear my cries
You were the role model for a slab of clay
That you left to harden when you went away*

*You created the life and planted the seed
Gave it no water, you left it to bleed*

It's sad to feel rejected, especially by someone that is supposed to be your guide in life. Many fatherless kids out there have felt

this way, too. But, they may not see the full picture. For me, I failed to see what God was doing for me in my life during those times I felt alone. I didn't see how He was filling in those gaps by placing men in my path to guide me... those 'Dads' that He called on for my rescue.

These men were neighbors, baseball coaches, teachers, church leaders, Grandfathers and a Stepdad – all placed in my life by God to help me. God did this for me. I didn't see it... until now.

Listen. A Dad can be more than the man that donated the 'bio-manjunk' that put us here. It can be any man that God has called to work in a child's life.

What Is A Dad's Job?

For men willing to take their role as a Dad seriously, it's a good idea to know what our responsibilities should be. What is a Dad's job?

This is a very good question. As men, we may think we already know the answer. But, what if we are wrong? What if those responsibilities we are doing every day are far from what we really should be doing as Dads? Because if we are doing it all wrong, our children will be affected.

I was young fella when my kids were born. Being in my early twenties, I had a job that I would go to every day to support my family. I was serious about my role as a husband and a new Dad because I wanted to be everything that my biological Dad was not. I made sure I reported to work on time every time. I rarely missed any days. It didn't matter if I was sick or not. I was always there.

There would be many times that I should have taken 'sick days', but I would force myself to go in anyway. I felt that I had to maintain my job so that I could support my family. I felt this was my most important duty as a husband and a Dad. If there's a chance to make some money, I was there. I was doing it for my family.

I remember many years ago, I would do things like cut grass or work odd jobs for people on the weekends to make some extra cash. Having extra money in the home can't hurt. On this one particular day, which happened to be on Father's Day, I was cutting grass for a lady. I didn't have a riding mower, so I used our push mower to do the job. It was hot outside and I was getting tired from pushing the mower, but I kept going. I was making money.

There was an area around the lady's pool that I was cutting. The grass was wet and there was a hill. Also, I wasn't wearing the appropriate shoes for the job. Let's just say that wearing sandals should never be worn when pushing a lawn mower. In a split second, I slipped on the hill and my right foot went under the mower. I released the emergency lever on the handle, but it was too late. I was in pain and I wasn't sure why.

Sitting on the grass, I managed to pull my foot out from under the mower. It felt like it had been hit by a sledge hammer. Well, after assessing the situation, I saw that my shoe was shredded, my foot was bleeding and my big toe was sorta dangling off to the side of my foot. It was ugly and time for a quick road trip to the local ER.

The lady rushed me to the hospital and the doctors started working on me. To make a long story short, I ended up spending the night there. The damage? Well, the mower managed to break four of my little toes and sliced half of my big toe right off. The doctors couldn't save it. On a positive note, I no longer have to worry about an ingrown toenail because there isn't one. And if I ever get a pedicure, I should qualify for a discount. Just sayin'.

The doctor told me to stay off my foot for a few weeks and to get some rest. Taking a few days off from work would do me some good, too. But, I didn't listen. My job and my duties were more important. I decided to take the prescribed pain pills, wrap my foot up with a bandage and I went on to work the next business day. Pretty stupid, huh?

The point in all of this is that 'work' was my number one priority. Even on a special day like Father's Day, I chose to work instead of spending time with my kids. It seemed like the right thing to do. People do it all the time. I mean, that's what men are supposed to do, right? Maybe not.

So, what is a Dad's job anyway?

Well, if we look at it from a worldly view and the things some of us have been taught in our own life, we would probably come up with a list like this:

World View Job #1
Dad's Work (Dad's Put Bread On The Table)

Many men, like myself, feel comfortable by working as part of their roles as Dads and husbands. It's a very important job, and in many cases, men are able to make more money than women in the workplace, so it's more sensible for the man to work. Plus, it's an activity that we feel more adequate doing because we get to use our minds and our strength, even though changing diapers and making a baby's formula requires it, too. For a man, it just seems more natural to apply it in the 'working world'.

Our forefathers from generations throughout our family tree always worked and provided for their families. The black and white photos of the men from our ancestry proved time and time again that callous hands was part of the role of being a Dad. So we learn from them and continue the tradition.

Even for those that believe in the Bible and what it says, we have always heard, "If a man don't work, he won't eat." And when you're raising a family, there are more mouths to feed. That means work harder and longer. Right? Working is, for most of us, our number one priority.

World View Job #2
Dad's Discipline Them (Only After The Mother Has Pulled Her Hair Out)

You know, we work all day. The last thing we want to do is come home and have to discipline our kids. That's the woman's job. Let her deal with it. But, we know there will come a time when we will have to get up from our recliner or stop that important thing we're doing to go on over and tend to our child. You know, our wife has been working at it for a couple of hours now and can't seem to make the kid act right. The noise is sorta distracting us from that important show we're trying to watch on cable. Yep, it's time to get up.

We proceed to the area where all of the noise is coming from and there's our 'out-of-control' child. Our wife is there, too. Her hair is a mess and it looks like she's been foaming at the mouth from all that screaming.

We do our 'Dad Duty' by creating the serious 'Daddy Face' and give our child the 'Daddy Crazy Eye'. I'm sure many of you have done this before. You basically lower your eyebrows and somehow make your eyes bigger at the same time. Some of us have gotten pretty good at this and added some extra cool stuff like the 'Eye Spasm' or the 'Glowing Red Face' and

'Shoulder Twitch'. We know that when our kids see all of this, they will know that we are serious. We can then proceed with disciplining them verbally in our 'Deep Man Voice', or for the Old Schoolers, we put them over our knee and spank their butts.

After we are finished and the whimpering slowly fades to silence, we then know we did our job. We can go back to our regularly scheduled program.

World View Job #3
Dad's Play With Them (When We Have The Time)
Most Dads enjoy playing with their kids. It could be because we like being able to go back in time in our minds and do the things we use to do in our youth. It's a lot of fun as long as our child wants to play the games that we want to play and how we want to play them.

I enjoyed playing baseball with my kids. I would stand at home plate with my bat and hit some grounders to them. After a few minutes of this, they would get bored and want to be the batters. This meant that I had to go play in the outfield and chase baseballs. The kids would never hit the ball directly to me. It was always in the opposite direction of where I was standing. Most of the time I had to run from the pitcher's mound to go play hind catcher. This got old quick, but I did it anyway. After a while, I would come up with an excuse of why we had to go back to the house.

Playing Tea Party with my daughter was kinda weird. I had to sit in a tiny chair and pretend to sip tea from an itty bitty cup. She would make me do it with my pinky finger sticking out. It made me feel a little uncomfortable, but being the awesome Dad that I wanted her to have, I did it anyway. I just hoped none of my male friends ever caught me playing.

I didn't have much time to play with my kids during the week. I worked and was pretty much tired when I got home. I just wanted to sit down, eat and relax. This didn't stop my kids from bugging me to death to play with them. This may have been the reason I made sure they had the latest video game equipment and the coolest games. It kept them occupied while I relaxed.

The weekends were different. In my early parenting days, this was our family time. We would always find something to do. We had places to go to and things to see. Plus, back then, I had the energy to keep up. We would take them to amusement parks, the zoo, the movies and other cool places. We would even take them roller skating and join in on the fun. I always thought I was being a cool Dad. You know, the kind of Dad that every kid wished they had.

Sadly, the years pass. The demand for our time from our kids seemed to dwindle away. They became content with doing their own thing like playing video games in their room with those music players in their ears. Or they sat around in their own little world texting on their phones to anybody and everybody in the world. They mostly liked staying on the computer doing whatever kids do; downloading junk or doing a search for stuff. Sometimes, as parents, we would sneak a peak from their bedroom doorway to make sure they were still breathing. Since they were quiet and looked OK, we kept on moving. It's just how kids were, so we didn't question it.

As responsible Dads, we know the importance of playing with
our kids. It builds a bond and memories that last forever.
Unfortunately, we're a little short on time to do it or the kids are
usually busy doing their own thing. Plus, we think they probably
could care less anyway, so we don't bother.

World View Job #4
Dad's Should Always Be There (Mostly Physically Because We Do Have A Lot On Our Minds)

We live in a busy world. Things are
happening around us at a super fast
pace. To keep up with the Jones',
you have to be on top of the game.
Technology is always coming up
with new gadgets and better ways
of doing things. You've got new
washing machines and dryers that
play music when they're finished
with a load. Or how about the new
TV's? They're bigger, more flatter
and you can even hang them on
your wall like a picture frame. In the
world of computers, you can now
surf the Internet on just about
anything; laptops, kneetops (such as

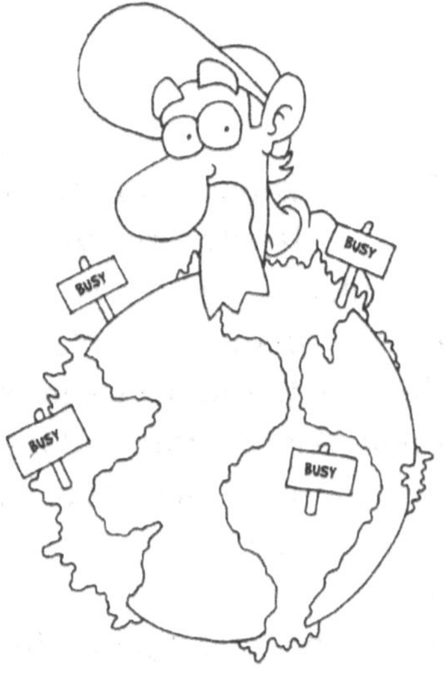

Kindle and iPads) and you can even surf up stuff on your phones.
All of this is great and a technological breakthrough, but it can be
expensive. Its purpose is to make our life better, but it comes
with a price. It involves more money and us giving more of our
time to work so that we can afford it. Then, of course, we have
our debt that keeps piling up with it's due date reminders. They
make it so easy for us to just 'swipe a card' when we are at the

store buying something. Many of us think we're using real money and forget that we're borrowing it from somewhere else. And in the home, it seems like everything around us needs some kind of repair work done to it. Fixing it with duct tape and Super Glue only lasts for a little while. All of this and many other things could explain why many of us are stressed. We suffer from a mental overload.

But, as responsible Dads, we know the importance of being there for our children. It could be that we have seen the negative results of children not having a Dad-figure in their home. It could also be that we know firsthand what it feels like from our own experience and we've made the decision of not doing the same thing to our kids. But, in life, we must prioritize everything and spending time with our kids does rank as one of those priorities. However, we think our 'physical' presence with them accomplishes this while our mind does it's own thing. Even though our 'body' may be in the same room as our kid, our brain wanders off into the realm of Everywhere Land.

I think everyone has developed the technique of multi-tasking. With so much going on in our life, we have developed the ability to take on more and juggle it like clowns at a circus. When it comes to listening to our kids, we can be in the same room looking them straight in the eye while they speak to us and still be able to calculate things in our minds or plan activities for the next day. Yeah, we may not hear everything our child is telling us, but we have learned to listen for vocal tone changes that signals us to nod or simply say 'yes' and an occasional 'no'. This keeps them satisfied that we are truly listening. Of course, when they become teenagers, they can see right through us. They know we aren't listening and ask, "Did you hear me?" or they will snap their fingers in front of our face to help us stay focused.

But, we are there for them.... physically. They will just have to know that we are still working on the mental part. It could take a while.

World View Job #5
Dad's Give Them Things To Do (To Keep Them Busy)

Kids are genetically wired to be constantly moving and getting

into something. That's why children left alone for a short period of time tends to lead into total destruction in whatever area we leave them. Think about it. A kid's bedroom is always the messiest room in the house. Leave a kid in a freshly cleaned play room for an hour and see what happens. It won't stay clean very long. I can guarantee you that.

As responsible Dads, we know the importance of making good use of that youthful energy. Most of the time, we use it to our advantage by giving them chores. We build them up with the idea that they can earn a whole whopping $2.00 if they complete our week's worth of duties. We might even pay them in pennies so that it will look like they've earned a ton of money for all of their hard work. And then we may come up with a story of how valuable

a dollar is and how 'the sky's the limit' on what they can spend it on. All of this may work up until they turn teenagers. Then we'll have to come up with another strategy.

The point in all of this is that we give them something to do and pay them for doing it. It teaches them good work ethics and builds character. It also cuts down on our own personal chore list and gives us more time to do the things we want to do. In our minds, it's worth the investment.

World View Job #6

Dad's Give Them Money (Regardless If They Earned It Or Not)
Kids have needs or so they say. As responsible Dads, we want to make sure our child has everything we didn't have growing up. We may think that, by giving them money, it will somehow make them better people. Making them earn it may be more trouble than what it's worth considering they would probably do a bad job on the chore we gave them anyway. This would create more work for us in the long run because we would have to fix what

they messed up. The easy thing to do would be to simply give them the money. Less work – less hassle. Right?

As long as our kids are happy, we are fulfilling our duties as responsible Dads. A smiling kid is visible proof that we are doing our jobs correctly. They will learn valuable life lessons like 'the good life comes for free', 'if you wait long enough for something, eventually someone will give it to you' or 'money falls from the sky – just hold your hand out'. These are awesome lessons that our kids can carry on to their adult life.

World View Job #7
Dad's Should Be A Good Role Model
As responsible Dads, we know that our children will learn how to become outstanding adults by simply watching us. The golden rule is 'if Dad does it, it must OK'. Unless of course, we disapprove of it. This is usually followed by us saying, "Do as I say, not as I do. Got it?" We may also inform them that some of the things we do can only be done when the child gets older and preferably moved out of the house so that we won't have to see them do it.

Our kids see our bad habits and actions. Sometimes they will say and do them, too. So, we try our best not to do them when they are around. To maintain our image as a good role model, we may scold them for it, unless they do it in a funny way. Then, we all laugh and consider it family entertainment.

It can be confusing at times for the child, but as Dads, we call the shots and have no problem helping them to understand. I think as long as we point out to them all of our good traits, they will be more focused on them instead and become better adults in the future.

World View Job #8

Dad's Show Them The Exit Door When They're Eighteen (And Help Them Pack Their Bags, Send Them On Their Way And Allow Them To Occasionally Come Back Home For A Visit, But More Often When The Grand Kids Are Born)

Having kids is great. They bring a lot of joy. Even though we've had to endure the many years of trouble, sorrow and stress. The overall picture of having them has been wonderful. I believe, as

Dads, we know that one day they will leave the nest. From the moment they were conceived into this world, we knew that time would fly by so fast and our kids would one day move out and start families of their own. For some of us, we started counting the days from Day One.

Eighteen years seems to be the magic number. At this age, our child has had enough time to learn everything from us they need to know about life, what's right and wrong and how to survive in this big crazy world. This is why we have pushed them so hard in school and at home. This is the reason for all of the long years of training we provided. If they need to know anything else, they can learn it on their own from a place called Hard Knocks. It's a special place that life provides for those needing more instruction. We've all been there.

At the ripe age of eighteen is when we get to see how well we did with our parenting skills. We finally get to see them soar with the wings of eagles that we glued feathers on. Now that they're eighteen. It's going to be a great day.

I know it's hard for some folks to see their kids leave the nest. Moms are usually the ones to break down in tears because their little baby has now become a grownup. That's why, as responsible Dads, we are usually the ones to help our kids follow through with the whole moving process. We help them pack their bags and show them the 'exit' door. We're happy to do it.

I know that sounds kinda mean, but we already made preparations. It's not like we're just throwing them off at the curb. A few years prior to this moment, we encouraged our child to get off the couch, to put down those video game controllers and get a job, taught them how to save their money, helped them buy a car that they worked hard for and even showed them how to find a home for rent in the Classified Section of our local newspaper. We had a purpose for all of that and now they're eighteen and ready to go. We're ready for them to go, too.

This is a proud moment. There in the driveway is our grown child sitting in their car loaded with all of their personal belongings. They are minutes away from venturing out on their own to face the world and they are equipped with everything we've taught them. We leave them with one more final salutation:

"Don't come back, unless it's for an occasional visit and maybe around the holidays like Christmas and Thanksgiving. Let us know when our grand baby is born, so that we can increase your number of visits. Oh, and before I forget... I love you!"

After all of our kids have left the nest, it is now time for Mom and Dad. The parenting days are officially over and real living can begin. This means we will have more money to spend, have less noise in the house and we will be able to take more vacations. It's freedom and we still have enough youth left in us to enjoy it. So, let's live it up! Right?

I know this isn't all of the duties we have as Dads according to a worldly view, but it does make up most of it. Our purpose was to hopefully make something awesome out of those kids we put here. It may seem like we treated them like milk in a refrigerator that has reached it's expiration date, but that's how it goes in life.

The whole parenting thing has been tough, but we survived and did pretty good considering we didn't really have any prior training in Dadmanship. Now our full grown child/adult can pass on to their children everything we've taught them. I'm sure they will improvise it based on what's going on in their world at the time. They will learn from any mistakes that we've made and will parent their children with their new changes.

When holidays come around, I'm sure our kids will remind us of all the mistakes we made. Everyone will laugh and have a wonderful time reminiscing about the good ol' days. Unless of course, if we did a terrible job in our parenting, we may never see our kids again. The trauma that we created for eighteen years may cause them to hate us. We may be the last people they will ever want to see. We will be blamed for their mental scars and the reason they go to a psychiatrist once a week.

But, that's how it goes sometimes in life. All you can do is keep on keepin' on. You know?

Does The Bible Say What A Dad's Job Is? Yep, It Does!

God knows the struggles we will have when it comes to parenting. That's why we have the Bible. If you ever need instructions on just about anything in life, the Bible should be the first place to look. Unfortunately for many of us, it's usually the last place we will check. And the reason we even looked at it was because it was our last resort after everything else we've tried had failed. But you know, all of that time and energy could have been saved if we had read the Bible from the start.

The Bible is a great source of information. It's God's handbook to us that will help us through life. It won't give us instructions on how to program our TV. It doesn't provide insight on how to repair a big block engine in a Chevy truck. But, if you have questions on how to live productively and peacefully, then the Bible is the place to look.

If you want to save your marriage, seek God and His Word. If you want to survive through hard economic times, seek God and His Word. If you want to prevent your child from turning into a little hoodlum, seek... well, you know.

When it comes to instructions on how to be a Dad, we can use the information the world freely provides. Some of it may have some truth in it. Who knows? We could follow the examples of many of the Dads out there in this world, but based on statistics and how kids act these days, I'm wondering if the world even knows what it's talking about.

God created this world. He created the people that live on it. He also created the 'man and woman' relationship and gave them reproductive organs that fit together to produce offspring. He had a purpose for all of it. It is all by His design. He even gave us the Bible to help us figure out what His purpose is for the family unit.

The Bible is a guideline for those of us that have chosen to turn away from sin and follow Jesus. We are Christians because we realized that our sin had separated us from God and we prayed to Him for forgiveness. We put our trust in Jesus for our Salvation. As Christian Dads, we should put our trust in Him to help us learn how to raise our children properly.

What does the Bible say about Dads? How should a Dad act and what are his job duties? Most of what I found from studying the Bible is how we are supposed to direct, discipline, encourage, love and teach them. Also, that love should be our main reason for all that we do for kids. Here's what I found:

Direct Them

Train up a child in the way he should go: and when he is old, he will not depart from it. - Proverbs 22:6

We are to give our kids direction. Hopefully, we are putting them on a positive path. They are influenced by our actions and look up to us for the 'road map'. It's best if we are following Jesus because He knows where He is going.

Discipline Them

He that spareth his rod hateth his son: but he that loveth him chasteneth him betimes. - Proverbs 13:24

Foolishness is bound in the heart of a child; but the rod of correction shall drive it far from him. - Proverbs 22:15

Withhold not correction from the child: for if thou beatest him with the rod, he shall not die. Thou shalt beat him with the rod, and shalt deliver his soul from hell. - Proverbs 23:13, 14

Discipline is important. According to the Bible, if you don't correct your child for doing wrong when they're young, it's going to hurt them down the road when they get older.

Kids do stupid things and we should expect it. Remember, we discipline them because we love them, not because they make us angry.

Encourage Them

And, ye fathers, provoke not your children to wrath: but bring them up in the nurture and admonition of the Lord. - Ephesians 6: 4

Fathers, provoke not your children to anger, lest they be discouraged. - Colossians 3: 21

Kids need encouragement because it keeps them motivated. When they do something that is totally awesome, we should tell them. They need the positive feedback.

Love Them

Charity suffereth long, and is kind; charity envieth not; charity vaunteth not itself, is not puffed up, doth not behave itself unseemly, seeketh not her own, is not easily provoked, thinketh no evil; rejoiceth not in iniquity, but rejoiceth in the truth; beareth all things, believeth all things, hopeth all things, endureth all things. Charity never faileth. - 1 Corinthians 13: 4-8a

The word charity means love. As Dads, everything we do for our child should be done out of love for them. Love is more than just a hug and a kiss. According to the scriptures, it will involve:

Patience
Kindness
Being free of envy
No prideful boasting
Honor
No self-seeking motives
Being slow to anger
Not keeping records of any wrong
Staying away from evil
Truth
Protection
Trust

Hope
Endurance
Never giving up

Teach Them

And these words, which I command thee this day, shall be in thine heart: And thou shalt teach them diligently unto thy children, and shalt talk of them when thou sittest in thine house, and when thou walkest by the way, and when thou liest down, and when thou risest up. And thou shalt bind them for a sign upon thine hand, and they shall be as frontlets between thine eyes. And thou shalt write them upon the posts of thy house, and on thy gates. - Deuteronomy 6: 6-9

We are to teach our children. This involves some one-on-one. As Dads, we have to make time to spend with them.

According to the Bible, our role as a Dad is a serious one. God has given us the responsibility of directing the paths of these wired-up little people that seem to starve for our attention. From the moment they are born, our job is basically to help them become outstanding citizens by planting them firmly on a foundation of Christian values in a world that's going downhill fast. And it's not going to get any better any time soon.

Here's what I received from the Bible concerning our job duties as Dads:

God's View Job #1
Dad's Teach Their Kids To Know About God And His Word

Planet Earth is a temporary place. One of these days, all of this material stuff that we have gotten used to seeing every day is going to be gone. The Bible warns us about it and tells us to

49

prepare for it. So, while we are here, we should be focusing more of our attention to the eternal stuff.

Here's the deal. Through Jesus Christ, we are promised eternal life:

For the wages of sin is death; but the gift of God is eternal life through Jesus Christ our Lord. - Romans 6:23

First, as Dads, we should make sure our life is squared up with the Lord. If not, we need to make things right. If you have never surrendered your life to Him, I would do that today. Secondly, we should make sure we share the memo with our family members – especially our kids. We have to teach them about God.

And this is life eternal, that they might know thee the only true God, and Jesus Christ, whom thou hast sent. - John 17:3

Eternal life begins by knowing God. Teaching our kids about Him should be our top priority. It would be great if we, as Dads, could have Bible studies with our children every day or at least once a week. But, the sad reality is that many of us don't take the time or that our day is filled with so much stuff that we don't have any time left. If we don't have time to read the Bible during the week for ourselves, how will we be able to take the time to teach it to our children? We can't and we don't.

The men in the old Bible days did. How they did it, I don't know. They may have been better organizers with their time. They may have rearranged their schedules so that there would be time for studying and teaching what they've learned to their children. They knew its importance and were building the foundation for their future generations.

In today's world, our priorities are mixed up and time is limited. This is another good reason why 'going to church' is needed in our life. Yeah, I know. You don't have to go to church to be a Christian, but to grow requires hearing from God's Word. If you're not doing it at home, church would be a great place to go where you can. We can learn and grow spiritually. Our kids can also learn about God. By taking our family to church, we will be building a strong spiritual foundation for everyone.

And these words, which I command thee this day, shall be in thine heart: And thou shalt teach them diligently unto thy children, and shalt talk of them when thou sittest in thine house, and when thou walkest by the way, and when thou liest down, and when thou risest up. And thou shalt bind them for a sign upon thine hand, and they shall be as frontlets between thine eyes. And thou shalt write them upon the posts of thy house, and on thy gates. - Deuteronomy 6: 6-9

One thing I've learned as a Dad is that we have to teach our children about God. If we don't, the world will and it doesn't have good things to say about Him. Actually, the world will make up stuff or poke fun and make Him appear to be a big joke. Even in school, our kids are being taught 'theories' of creation and evolution. They are believing that everybody evolved from monkeys and the world they live in was created from some kind of cosmic boom. It's our duty to teach them the truth.

God's View Job #2
Dad's Teach Their Kids To Be Like Jesus
The greatest commandment we are given from God is to love Him with all of our heart.

And thou shalt love the LORD thy God with all thine heart, and with all thy soul, and with all thy might. - Deuteronomy 6:5

As Dads, if we are truly keeping this commandment, then it will work it's way outward in everything we say and do. Our kids will see this lifestyle in us because the best way to teach our children to be like Jesus is to lead them by example.

We have to make sure we are truly doing what the Bible teaches us and living the same life that Jesus lived. Our kids will get mixed information if we take them to church and then allow them to see us act like a bunch of heathens during the week. They are watching us and taking mental notes.

And, ye fathers, provoke not your children to wrath: but bring them up in the nurture and admonition of the Lord. - Ephesians 6:4

Dads have the responsibility of being the leaders of their families. This is a big job. We teach our children by sharing what the Bible says and by showing them how it applies through our own life.

Jesus isn't popular in today's world in the eyes of many children these days. It's mostly because of what they see and hear in the world. There are too many TV shows that make a mockery of Christianity. There are some songs being played on those harmless MP3 players that warp a child's fragile little mind. There are also people out there that claim to be Christian role models that are acting totally different than what the Bible says a Christian should be. It's a messed up world we live in. But, if we set the standards of living with the model that Jesus left us to follow, we will be producing some awesomely cool traits in our kids.

Here's an example of a ministry that's actually doing it:

Accelerated Christian Education (ACE) is an American educational products company which produces Christian-based school curriculum to over 7,000 schools. By using the Bible in its educational curriculum, it claims to be producing the following 60 traits from Jesus' life in its students:

Appreciative
Attentive
Available
Committed
Compassionate
Concerned
Confident
Considerate
Consistent
Content
Cooperative
Courageous
Creative
Decisive
Deferent (showing respect)
Dependable
Determined
Diligent
Discerning
Discreet
Efficient
Equitable
Fair
Faithful
Fearless
Flexible
Forgiving
Friendly
Generous
Gentle
Honest
Humble
Joyful
Kind
Loyal
Meek
Merciful
Observant
Optimistic
Patient
Peaceful
Perseverant (being persistent)
Persuasive
Prudent
Punctual
Purposeful
Resourceful
Respectful
Responsible
Secure
Self-controlled
Sincere
Submissive
Tactful
Temperate
Thorough
Thrifty
Tolerant
Truthful
Virtuous

Yeah, I know. I borrowed this information from a website. But the fact is, by simply teaching our kids the values that Jesus left for us from His life, it can help them become better people in the real world. They can have better ethics, values and morals — which is something the world really needs right now. It's best to begin while they're young.

Like I said earlier, our kids watch our lives. They learn from our actions. If we reflect Jesus to them, they can benefit. And just like Jesus did when He walked the Earth, he spent some one-on-one time with His disciples. He was training them – teaching them.

We can do the same with our children through any activity we

want to share with them. A fishing trip is more than teaching them how to get their own food. It's an opportunity for conversations that can teach them any of the traits about Jesus listed above. The same applies to throwing a baseball with them. It doesn't have to be about building strength in their arms. It can be more than that.

When we are living for the Lord and using love as our motive to be with our kids, God can use this opportunity to help them grow. We are fulfilling our duty in teaching them to be more like Jesus.

God's View Job #3
Dad's Get Their Kids Prepared For The World
For this cause shall a man leave his father and mother, and shall

*be joined unto his wife, and they two shall be one flesh. -
Ephesians 5: 31*

One thing I have learned as a parent is that kids grow up so fast. It seems like yesterday I was changing my kids' diapers. I blinked one day and then realized they now had lives of their own. Where did all of the time go?

We have a very short time to get our kids prepared for the world. There is so much for them to learn and we have to make time to teach it to them. So, what do they need to know from us?

Even though the Bible doesn't specify individual tasks that we should teach them, we have to use our common sense to decide what our child needs to know before they venture out on their own. What will they need to be able to survive in the world? We can use our experiences and the things we learned to share with them. Here are a few things I feel that every kid needs to know about before they leave the nest:

1. Dads Teach Them How To Live Out On Their Own
*Train up a child in the way he should go: and when he is old, he will not depart from it. -
Proverbs 22:6*

Living out on our own is more than just paying rent to someone. It's knowing what to do when we get out there.

For most kids, being out on

their own means freedom. And freedom can mean a number of things depending on how a child's brain thinks. It could be trying and doing things that weren't allowed when they were living at home. Or, it could mean freedom to apply everything they've learned from their parents and doing it in their own way. The difference in the two is that one is a rebellious attitude. It usually ends up with something bad happening that makes them plead and beg to come back home. And we don't want that to happen, do we?

What are the basics they need to know when living out on their own? Here's a few:

a. They Need To Know How To Cook
Kids need to know that there's more to cooking than simply popping Ramen noodles in a microwave. We have to teach them the importance of eating the right foods at the right times. You know... breakfast, lunch and dinner... and the five basic food groups.

If we allow our kids to eat 'fast foods' all the time and at any time they want during the day, we are going to have some issues. This could explain why there's an obesity problem in America. This leads into health issues. It's hard to live productive lives when your body can't function properly.

When they're young teenagers, we should show

them around the kitchen. Teach them why it's best to use utensils such as a fork, spoon and butter knife instead of their hands. Explain the use of a plate and why it's safer for everyone's health as compared to digging food out of Tupperware dishes from the refrigerator with their hands.

Allow them to learn to cook meals for the family with adult supervision. Show them the right way to cook by using frying pans, boilers and cooking sheets. And most importantly, teach them how to use a stove by putting a lot of emphasis on temperature settings on the burners and oven. The more they know, the better they'll grow. And learning to cook is for both girls and boys.

Keep this thought in mind. What if your son never gets married? Will they know how to cook for themselves? Or will they have to come back home to eat? I say teach them now so that they won't have to. Just sayin'.

b. They Need To Know How To Clean

To set the record straight, the phrase, "Cleanliness is next to Godliness", is not in the Bible. For hundreds of years, mothers have been using this phrase to get their children to clean their room. I'm not really sure where it came from. However, being clean and living in a clean environment is a good thing. I believe everyone should practice it. It helps us to stay healthy and organized. It also keeps the rats and roaches from taking over our homes.

Learning to clean begins when a child is young and it starts with their bedroom. I have tried to teach my kids the importance of keeping their rooms clean. I have used it as a life lesson of how our life performs better when there's no clutter and filth residing in it. Even though at the time it may have went in one ear and out the other, I think now, that they are older, they are finally getting it.

Having a clean room, or a clean home, simply makes life better and easier. It helps you stay organized, healthy and focused. It also offers a place that welcomes others to come in and hang out. Nobody wants to come to somebody's house and feel like they are visiting a landfill. It makes a person feel yucky when they leave. Plus, there are sanitary and health issues when it comes to eating and drinking from gross kitchenware. A person can catch cooties. If someone does come for a visit the first time to a nasty home, you can bet they won't come back again.

As Dads, we should encourage our kids to clean their room. As they grow older, we can add more responsibility to their plate by having them clean the bathroom, kitchen and living room. Cleaning isn't just for girls. Here again, what if your son never gets married? Will you or your wife make a special trip to his house to do their cleaning? The fact is, one day they will have to do it on their own in their own home or a health inspector will pay them a visit. We might as well start them early. This could prevent them from becoming hoarders in the future.

c. They Need To Know How To Do Laundry
Back in the old days, doing laundry involved a wash board and several hours of strenuous labor. I can't say that I remember those times personally, but I have heard about them. In today's

world, doing laundry is more easier than ever. These new hi-tech washing machines and dryers do all of the work for you. All you have to do is put the clothes in, add the soap and mash the GO button. It's pretty simple. Actually, the one we bought last year plays a sweet little tune to let you know it's done with the load. Isn't that cool?

But, regardless of how simple it is or how cool we think it might be, kids need to know how to do it because one day they will have to do it on their own. They also need to know that doing laundry is more than just washing and drying, it's also about folding and putting the clothes away.

There are a lot of kids out there that live out of clothes baskets in their bedroom. I mean, the clothes are clean, but they lay all crunched up in those baskets in the corner. What could be the problem with this? Well, people are given a bad impression of kids that wear wrinkled clothes. It doesn't look good. A good first impression is important when it comes to meeting people, especially during a job interview. Bosses tend to hire people that look serious about wanting to work. Nice looking clothes means a better chance of our kids getting a job... which means less chance of them having to move back home. You with me?

d. They Need To Know How To Find A Job
A lot has changed in this area when it comes to finding a job. Back in my day, all you had to do was find a job ad, visit the place

of business, fill out an application and wait for the phone call. Now it's all done over the Internet or through a job placement service.

As Dads, we should walk our kids through this new process — even if we have to learn it ourselves. Work with them on how to fill out those online applications and help them create a resume. I'm sure there's a new modern way of doing that, too. We just need to figure it out.

We can also show them another purpose of all of those social networking websites such as Facebook, Twitter and whatever else is out there. By teaching them to reach out to their friends that have jobs or companies that are hiring, the whole 'social networking' experience can be more than just playing games and posting stupid stuff as status updates. It could be a way for them to generate job leads and actually landing one.

e. They Need To Know How To Budget And Manage Their Finances
Hopefully, our kids did well in Basic Math. If not, they could be in trouble. They may have hated taking it in school, but here is where it will be used — in their finances. Handling money involves basic math skills. It's best that they know how to add, subtract, multiply and divide. Maybe we can buy them a calculator for Christmas. They will be using Basic Math for the rest of their

lives.

But my God shall supply all your need according to his riches in glory by Christ Jesus. - Philippians 4:19

Even though God will supply our needs, He may do it through our income. He also expects us to be good stewards with what He's given us. This means setting budgets and not overspending. As Dads, we should teach our kids this important life principle. The last thing we want to happen is for them to go broke and have to move back home along with their wife and ten children. It won't be a pretty picture.

We could start out when they are young by showing them the value of a dollar. We can teach them how to spend it (and to count their change) and how to save for something they want. When they get older and are able to earn some money, we can help them start a savings account and help them keep records of their investment.

We could also get them involved in our personal finances and show them how we do it from month to month. This way they will know what to expect when they get out on their own.

f. They Need To Know How To Use Basic Tools
I believe every kid – boys and girls - should know how to use basic tools around the house, This includes a hammer, screwdrivers, wrenches, sockets, duct tape, WD40 and some of the cool stuff they offer in the tool aisle at Wally World.

There will be many times when our kids, living on their own, will need to know how to fix something. Things do break and many of those times it's an easy fix. Knowing how to tighten up a screw or bolt could save them hundreds of dollars in service calls.

With today's technology, if a kid learned how to use basic tools, they could do a search on YouTube for the repair needed and would be able to follow along and do it themselves. As Dads, we could teach them to become independent do – it - yourselfers. Wouldn't that make us proud?

We could start their training when they are younger by allowing them to watch us do repairs. As we work on something, we could introduce them to the tools we're using and calling each one out by name.

"This is a screwdriver. See the funny looking star shape? That makes it a Phillips head screwdriver. The other one is slotted. See the straight line?"

Over time, we could ask them to go and fetch a tool that we needed and they would know exactly the one to get.

"Hey, go get me that 9/16 box wrench. It's next to the ball ping hammer and needle nose pliers."

"Got it! Here ya go, Dad!"

Working on home projects

with your child is always fun and educational. It builds a bond with them and creates memories that the both of you will keep forever.

g. They Need To Know How To Communicate

You would think, with all of these technological devices, kids would know how to communicate with each other. If you look around you, all you see is kids on their cell phones, not using their mouths but their thumbs. They're texting. Say what? And if you look closer, none of it makes any sense. It's kinda weird.

For example, if something is funny, kids don't say, "Wow! That was a funny thing you just said." Instead, they text, "LOL (Laughing Out Loud)." or "ROTFLMBO (Rolling On The Floor Laughing My Butt Off)." I guess if something was really funny, they would use the second example. Take a look at your child's text conversation with one of their friends. It's a very strange way of communicating.

The problem is when they get into a social setting with real people and real places. They don't know how to act or what to say. Many times they simply shy away. They tend to run from personal confrontations.

Back in my day, we used telephones. We actually called people and had real conversations. When the phone call was over, we would actually go outside and have more conversations with people in person. This was an every day event.

We didn't 'text' people like kids do today. The only thing that might come close to today's 'texting' is when we decided to write someone a letter. This involved a pencil and a piece of paper. This was a form of communication that seems to have long been forgotten. Do kids even know how to write a letter these days? Probably not.

In school, teachers would make us stand in front of the class and give verbal presentations. It was scary, but it taught us how to speak to people. I think kids these days do Power Point presentations where they do all of the work on a computer and show it on a screen like a video slideshow and sorta hide out to the side where no one can see them. It's not the same.

As Dads, we need to go back to the basics. We may need to get our kids off those techo-devices that keeps them secluded in their rooms. Let's get them outdoors where the real people are and encourage conversations. Introduce them to a telephone and give them a sheet of paper and a pencil and make them communicate with it to their grandparents. Their grandparents would love receiving a letter from the grand kids and our kids could learn something from the experience, too.

When our child is grown and living on their own, they will need to know how to communicate with people and many of them won't accept text messages. Ordering pizza, contacting your landlord to inform them that you're going to be late with the rent, getting a roofer to fix a leak on your roof and contacting 911 for a real life crisis are all done better with a telephone call – not a text message. Dads, we need to teach them how it's done.

h. They Need To Know How To Be Responsible, Accountable and Committed

Kids need to know that there are consequences for their actions. Just like when they were younger, there are penalties for doing something wrong and rewards for doing something right.

If our young child steals a piece of candy from a store, we should march them back in there and make them return it and apologize. Then spank their butts for stealing. It's wrong! If you don't, they'll think it's OK. When they do it when they're older, they will go to jail and have a record as a thief. This doesn't look good on a job application.

If you walk into your house and notice that a vase is broken, you ask your kids, "Who did this?" and no one speaks up, you punish all of them. Later, the guilty one will get jumped on by the other ones. He will learn the hard way to take responsibility for his actions the next go around.

If you tell your child to do something and he doesn't, you punish them. He will learn to be accountable for his decision to disobey. Next time, I bet he will be committed to doing what you tell him.

On a positive note, if our child takes it upon himself to cut grass while we're at work without being told and we know that it was done out of good intentions, we should reward him by surprising him with some money or a gift.

This is how we teach our kids. It's through teaching and discipline. We have to let them know that there are consequences for their actions whether it's good or bad. This will help them when they are older when it comes to any decision they will ever have to make. They will consider the outcome.

2. Dads Equip Them With The Tools To Perform Their Life's Work

What will our child be when they grow up? I know we started asking this question as soon as our child popped out of the womb. We've always looked at them for some special characteristic that would give us some insight into their future career. Am I right?

If he comes out all chunky, we might say, "Yep. He's going to be a football player."

Or, if it's a girl and she comes out screaming, we might say, "Aww! How sweet. Listen to that wonderful set of lungs. I bet she's going to be an opera singer one day."

All through their life we look for signs. We observe their interests and watch for something that will set them apart from everyone else. Don't worry. It's normal. Actually, I think it's part of God's plan for parents. We naturally want what's best for our children, so we look for special characteristics from them. If we see something special, we can then help them by setting them on a successful path for their future.

If ye then, being evil, know how to give good gifts unto your children, how much more shall your Father which is in heaven give good things to them that ask him? - Matthew 7: 11

To help them get prepared for the working world, we look for things they love doing. The best job to have is one that you actually enjoy going to every day. Many people have settled with their 'dead end' job because they have given up on pursuing what they would enjoy doing. Or, in their earlier years, they didn't receive the encouragement or direction from their parents.

If our child shows an interest in helping others, we could begin by getting them involved in charity groups so that they gain experience. This could lead them to a career in the medical field or any area that involves customer service, like working in the Returns Department at Wally World. That would be a rewarding job for anybody's child.

If they enjoy dancing, we could sign them up for dance classes. This could prepare them for their future job on Broadway or as a backup dancer for the latest music sensation. Every time our child made a big paycheck or appeared on TV, we could remind them that we played a part in making that happen.

I hope you get the idea. Basically, we have to look for those special traits that our kid has and help them to improve them. We should direct their path to help them take these gifts to higher levels and on to a potential career. If it involves college or tech school, help them get there.

3. Dads Get Them Prepared To Do God's Work

For Christians, our biggest job is to share the Gospel. Jesus gave everyone this assignment and it's something we all should take very seriously.

Go ye therefore, and teach all nations, baptizing them in the name of the Father, and of the Son, and of the Holy Ghost: teaching them to observe all things whatsoever I have commanded you: and, lo, I am with you alway, even unto the end of the world. Amen. - Matthew 28: 19, 20

As Dads, it's important that we let our kids know that they have this assignment, too. God has called us all to do something for Him. He has given us the tools – through our gifts and talents - to use for His glory. That special talent that your child has is what God gave him or her for that purpose. Dads need to recognize this and help their child to develop it, knowing that the ultimate purpose is to use it for the Lord.

Have you ever wondered why some kids are gifted with the ability to sing, draw, play music or help others? Each of these gifts were given to them by God to use for Him.

As Dads, we should teach our kids the importance of doing ministry and how important their role is in doing Kingdom work. We should help our child grow spiritually by being an example of Jesus through our actions, teach them from the

Bible and by taking them to church so that they can learn more about Him.

We can also help our child perfect those gifts the Lord has given them by providing the tools they will need to make them better. Young musicians need instruments, young artists need artistic essentials and young singers need a place to perform. It's all for the glory of God. Whatever gift our child has, we should do our part to nurture it.

Being A Dad Should Be A Reflection Of Our Father In Heaven

Before life existed, God was building molds of what He wanted everything to look like. It took Him 6 days to create everything – night and day (Day 1), the sky (Day 2), the land, sea and vegetation (Day 3), the sun, moon and stars (Day 4), all of the living creatures in the sea, in the air and on the land (Day 5)...

and on the sixth day, he created man and woman.

Day 6 was kinda special. God had already made everything else and wanted his next creation to be very personal to Him. He decided to make man and woman in His own image. Can you imagine that?

So God created man in his own image, in the image of God created he him; male and female created he them. - Genesis 1: 27

From the very beginning of time, man was meant to reflect God. To have the image of God, it would include having His characteristics that we discussed earlier. Keep in mind, man was first created in a world without sin, so he may have been a mirror-image of God. But, when man sinned, his character began falling away. And it's been falling ever since.

But your iniquities have separated between you and your God, and your sins have hid his face from you, that he will not hear. - Isaiah 59: 2

A life separated from God is dead. Thankfully, God sent Jesus to bridge the gap between man and Himself.

For God so loved the world, that he gave his only begotten Son, that whosoever believeth in him should not perish, but have everlasting life. For God sent not his Son into the world to

When people accept Jesus into their hearts, they are being reconnected to God. This is why people say, "I've been saved." It is because they have been 'saved' from spiritual death. They now have 'eternal' life through Jesus.

For Dads out there, it's best to be reconnected to God. It allows us to be molded to be more like Jesus and to help us to develop His characteristics. It helps us to be more of a positive influence to our children and to become better Dads. Who would know better than Almighty God himself? He is called Abba several times in the Bible because Abba means 'father'.

For ye have not received the spirit of bondage again to fear; but ye have received the Spirit of adoption, whereby we cry, Abba, Father. The Spirit itself beareth witness with our spirit, that we are the children of God: - Romans 8: 15, 16

The closer we walk with Jesus, the more we become like Him. And if 'being a Father' is one of His attributes, then we know we are heading in the right direction. You agree?

Some Common Mistakes Made By Dads

Parenting isn't easy and we all are going to make mistakes. Raising kids will put our emotions through the test and we may do things that we will later regret. That's just how it goes.

For example, as I am writing this paragraph, my two youngest daughters are out of school for the Summer and running crazy through the house. They are loud and it's hard for me to even think. I am tempted to get angry and throw this laptop across the room at them. But, before I react on my emotions, I have to stop and think it through. For one, my actions may destroy this expensive laptop that I'm working on and everything I have typed on it for the past few days will be lost. Secondly and most importantly, it will be very hard for me to explain to my wife and DFACS why my kids have pop-knots on their heads.

Being a Dad involves wisdom that only God can give. It takes love and time to consider how our actions will affect our children. I have listed five mistakes that Dads are known to make when it comes to raising their children. I'm sure there are others but these seem to be the most common. Let's take a look:

Losing Our Temper

Wherefore, my beloved brethren, let every man be swift to hear, slow to speak, slow to wrath: for the wrath of man worketh not the righteousness of God. - James 1: 19, 20

I'm sure everyone has gotten angry a time or two. I know I have. If you have children, there's almost a guarantee that they are going to do something that's going to make you mad.

Out of all of the times I have ever been angry, 90% of those times were directed toward my children. It could be because of something they did or something they said. Or, it could be because I may have had a bad day and needed someone to vent it on. Since my short wife doesn't take any crap off of me, I may have vented it off on them instead. They're young and can take it.

Getting angry is a normal reaction. The problem is in how we react to anger, especially when we lash out and get all crazy. We usually say and do things that we will later regret. We will need some self-control and the ability to recognize it when we get to the boiling point. We may have to stop and walk away from certain situations. We might have to count to ten... or even up to a thousand.

Not Having Time To Listen To Them

Life is busy and we probably have tons of 'data' floating around in our Mind Space. We have places to go to and things to do. But, in the end, it's the time we've spent with our kids that's more important. Creating bonds and memories with them have more lasting value. Sometimes it takes us longer in life to realize this fact.

I'm guilty of not listening to my kids. I have always blamed it on my A.D.D. (Attention Deficit Disorder). Even though I have never been diagnosed by a doctor with it, I assumed that since I can't seem to focus on anything very long, it must be what it is. If it turns out to be 'selective hearing' like my wife thinks it is, then my brain chooses to focus only on conversations that it thinks is important. If that's the case, then I'm being selfish to think that my personal thoughts outweigh what my kids are wanting to share with me. That's wrong and I'm guilty.

I'm learning that if my child is willing to reach out to talk to me, I should make the time to listen. It's a special moment that can't be replaced. One day my child will be grown and will have busy lives of their own. They will be too busy for me.

Lecturing

Some of us are good speakers when it comes handling a family crisis. I always thought I was good at it, but realized I had it all wrong.

Let's say our child needs some advice. We step up to the invisible podium and give them a three hour speech. We may feel that its the appropriate thing to do. We address their problem and we look professionally concerned because we took three hours of our day to talk to them about it.

But the sad fact is, all we should have said was just a few words. Long speeches to our kids makes them not want to come to us with their problems. They will be afraid that it will turn into a lecture. It would be best if we could keep our words to a minimum and do more listening. This will allow them some time to communicate with us. The conversation can then flow back and forth.

Being Too Harsh On Them

A soft answer turneth away wrath: but grievous words stir up anger.- Proverbs 15: 1

Parents want to be heard. If we have a problem with our child, we want to make sure our kids hear us loud and clear. We lay down the law. We might get all up in their face; snarling and foaming at the mouth. This puts them into 'defense mode' and they start fussing back and being disrespectful. This causes us to get even louder and we start taking our belt off. We all know what happens next.

The Bible tells us a soft answer turns away wrath. If we talk calmly and sensibly with our children, we could get our point across and prevent all of the drama.

We could think of our child as a little plant that we are helping to grow. What would help the process of 'growth' move smoother? A severe tropical storm with thunder, lightning, gusty wind and hail? Or maybe a slight drizzling of rain and sunshine?

Not Making The Kids Realize That They Are Loved

My little children, let us not love in word, neither in tongue; but in deed and in truth. - 1 John 3: 18

We all need to be loved – our kids are included.

Most families have developed a routine of telling each other, "I love you." Many times it is at night before bed time or after a phone conversation. I know that's how we do things in my home. There's rarely a time that we don't say we love each other.

For kids feeling unloved, the problem could be that the words have become so 'routine'. It may lack a true feeling behind it when it's being said. After saying the same thing every day for several years, it's bound to lose its original sincerity. It may have become just another thing to say.

According to the scripture in 1 John 3: 18, love should be more of an 'action' word. That would mean that we would have to show it in the way we treat our kids. Here are a few ideas to put your love into action:

1. Spend some one-on-one time with each of your children. Take them out somewhere − just the two you − so that they can feel special.
2. Build their self-esteem and confidence in themselves by letting them know how proud you are of them. You could remind them of some of their accomplishments.
3. Try to find something positive in the things they do that you would normally fuss at them about. Like, "Hey, I'm beginning to like your new look − the dark thick eye liner you're using really brings out the color in your eyes."
4. Sit around with your child and watch old home videos (or look at old childhood photos) and tell them some of the things you remember about them. You could explain the details of why a particular photo of them was taken.
5. Tell them how good it is to be their parent and how happy

you are of the way they are growing up. Find things about them that make you happy
and tell them.

6. Have a play-day with them. Let them choose a game and play it together. Even if it's childish or something you don't even want to play, let them decide. Your purpose is to give of your time to them. That's what counts.

7. Learn more about them and their school. Find out who their friends and teachers are. Use this information for a later time  to ask them questions that pertain to their daily routine. "How was your day at school? Did you sit with Susie on the bus?" "Did Mrs Smith grade your English test yet?" These type of questions show them that you care for them personally and that you actually listen.

8. Talk to them with no distractions, even if it means cutting off cell phones, computers and televisions. It's easy to get distracted by everything around else. It's best to create a quiet atmosphere when talking with your child.

9. Eat dinner as a family and take turns talking about each others day. The dinner table is perfect for family bonding.

10. Compliment your child to your friends and do it so that your kid can overhear you. This lets them know you are serious.

11. Hug them, kiss them, and say 'I love you' every day... no matter what.

Being A Dad Is A Ministry
That Any Man Can Take Part In

Lo, children are an heritage of the LORD: and the fruit of the womb is his reward. - Psalms 127: 3

We should see our kids as gifts from God. And just like the worldly gifts we receive on our birthdays or around Christmas, we should be thankful and not toss them to the side. There are too many men out there doing that in the world today.

One of my most memorable family Christmas mornings was back when my son was around five years old. My kids were spoiled rotten because my wife and I have always pampered them with the easy life. We made it a point to buy them pretty much anything they ever wanted. This particular Christmas wasn't any different. Our tree was decorated with beautiful lights and filled with a bunch of gifts.

That year, I think my wife found a deal on some full-bodied pajamas for my son at our local superstore. She bought a bunch of them and wrapped them individually as gifts to put under our Christmas tree. When it came time for my kids to open them, I must have given my son five presents containing pajamas back to back. After opening the third box, he got mad and slung the gift across the room. He wanted toys and all he was opening was pajamas. This made me mad because he was being ungrateful, so I whooped him and said, "Hey, look! If you don't want them, I'll just give them to somebody else! I'm sure there's a kid out there somewhere that would love to have them."

In society today, I believe some children are being treated like unwanted presents. These 'unwanted' gifts from God are being tossed to the side just like pajamas given to a spoiled kid at Christmas time. That's when God steps in and gives these gifts to someone else.

When God gives us something, He expects us to take care of it. The reality is that He ultimately owns it and wants us to be good stewards of it. If He provides us with a home and a car, He wants us to keep it cleaned and maintained. We should be thankful and we show it in how we treat it. The same is true with the gift of children.

Being a steward is a servant-type job where we manage the property of someone else. Yes, this property is a gift to us because it's in our hands, but the rightful owner is the one that give it to us. As we serve as stewards of God's gifts, we are basically serving Him and He expects us to be faithful.

Moreover it is required in stewards, that a man be found faithful. - 1 Corinthians 4: 2

And whatsoever ye do, do it heartily, as to the Lord, and not unto men; - Colossians 3: 23

That's why I believe the act of being a Dad is more of a ministry than a self-serving role. It's similar to any other service we do for the Lord and to others because, as Dads, we are looking out for the well-being of the child. Here's what the word 'ministry' means:

Ministry is from the Greek word **diakoneo**, meaning 'to serve' or **douleuo**, meaning 'to serve as a slave'. In the New Testament, ministry is seen as service to God and to other people in His name. Jesus provided the pattern for Christian ministry - He came, not to receive service, but to give it.

Even as the Son of man came not to be ministered unto, but to minister, and to give his life a ransom for many. - Matthew 20:28

Ministry is more than sharing the Gospel of Jesus Christ. It's also about ministering to the physical, emotional, mental, vocational, and financial needs of others. I mean, this is what Jesus did. He is our example of what we should be doing, too.

In a situation where biological Dads have chosen to toss their gift aside, God has to step in and fill in the gaps. This is when He provides children with replacement male figures in their life. These men that step up are used by God to be the 'Dad' role models to help guide and teach them.

Pure religion and undefiled before God and the Father is this, to visit the fatherless and widows in their affliction, and to keep himself unspotted from the world. - James 1: 27

It's a ministry and a rescue mission created by God designed for the purpose of that child needing a Dad in his life. Who would God call for this task? It can be any man.

Stepdads
Adoptive Dads
Foster Dads
Father-Inlaws
Neighbors
And men that step up to the plate to be a mentor to a child

Say A Prayer

©2012 - A Modern Day Psalm by Jeff Todd

Verse 1
Let's say a prayer for the child
Who's away from home and running wild
Young runaway
No where to go
Don't forget the girl out on the street
Selling herself for food to eat
Young prostitute
Endless road

Chorus
Ask the Lord tonight to show these kids a better way
'cause the price in the end is a hell of a price to pay
Take them under Your wing and never leave them alone
Please watch them night and day and show them the way home

Verse 2
Let's say a prayer for the kid on crack
Whose life's astray, no turning back
Young drug user
Digging a hole
And that young boy whose mind went
When he took the lives of the innocent
Young murderer
On Death Row

Repeat Chorus

A Call To Action

If you look around the world today, whether it's on the news or on the Internet, you will see that there are many kids out there that are fatherless. Based on statistics, many of these kids will end up in places that they should have never been. They need male guidance – someone to lead them on a better path.

It's a serious situation that requires a 'call to action' to any man willing to take a stand.

To Biological Dads
God has given you a gift. The child you put here needs you. Take a stand today and be the Dad that you were called to be. Regardless of how the world has treated you, break the cycle and make a change in your child's life. Your courageous step will make a difference for them and their generations to come.

Pray and ask God to help you to become the man He expects from you. He can and He will.

To The Men
There are many children out there that need male role models in

their life. There is a desperate need for men to take a stand to lead, guide and direct them.

This is a call to action to stepdads, adoptive Dads, foster Dads, father-inlaws, male neighbors and mentors. If you are one of them or would like to become one, there are kids that need you.

Pray and ask the Lord to place a fatherless child in your path. You will be serving the Lord as you reach out to a child in need.

And the King shall answer and say unto them, Verily I say unto you, Inasmuch as ye have done it unto one of the least of these my brethren, ye have done it unto me. - Matthew 25: 40

Take a look around you. The Lord may have already placed a child within your reach. It could be in your home, in your family, in your neighborhood or at your local DFACS office.

Be courageous and make a stand today.

Have not I commanded thee? Be strong and of a good courage; be not afraid, neither be thou dismayed: for the LORD thy God is with thee whithersoever thou goest. - Joshua 1: 9

To The Children

If you're a child that feels all alone without a Dad, God says that He is a father to the fatherless. Look away from the

world for answers and turn to Him. God will begin working and sending men to your rescue. But first, let go of that hurt inside.

There is a call to action for you today. Tear down that wall you built around your heart and watch God as He works in your life.

What Does It Mean to Be A

Christian

Written and illustrated by Jeff Todd

Introduction

The guidelines for Christian living have already been written. You can find everything you need to know right there in God's Holy Word - The Bible. It's just a matter of opening it up and reading it. The Spirit of God will reveal to you the things you need to know and give you the ability to understand them.

The purpose of this book is not to be a substitute for reading the Bible. Oh no! Everyone should read it. My hope and intentions for writing this book is that it will inspire you, as the reader, and will offer humorous illustrations to use in your walk with Christ and to put Christianity out there in an easy to understand format. Together we can learn to live our life to the fullest with happiness and joy that God intended for us to live.

First of all, being a Christian doesn't have to be boring and dull. I believe it should be energetic and alive. We are to be a light in the world that we live in and shine out to others. When a person sees the way we are, it should make them want to be that way, too.

Our lifestyle should point them to Jesus. Everything we say and do should reflect the One that saved us.

I have never considered myself to be like everyone else. The way I look at life may be different than the way others see it. Even as a young child, Christian people to me were always the suit and tie-wearing folks or the snooty ladies wearing the dresses and they acted very *'stiff necked'*. It was almost like they were afraid to smile.

I agree, it was wrong of me to segregate Christians like this, but those were the Christians I knew. As I grew older, I realized that not all Christians were like this and were actually normal people.

Being called into the ministry, I have to use what the Lord has given me. This includes the relationship I have with Jesus through His grace that saved me, His Word, and the gifts, talents, and characteristics that He gave me.

When you put that all together in a mixing bowl, you have:

I know from experience that being a Christian isn't a difficult task. It's not a series of rituals or following a magic formula. It's actually so simple that anyone could do it.

That's my purpose and focus of writing this book! I want to write something that would minister to people (no matter who they were) and possibly help them understand what being a Christian is all about.

It's got to be simple and easy to understand. I don't use BIG words when I speak, so why should I write BIG words when I am using this to reach people and lead them to Jesus. I can't! It's not how God made me!

If you're reading this today, this book is for you from a simple minded person like me. Being a Christian is awesome and it's not as weird as you may have heard. We're not crazy people! If you have never asked Jesus to come into your life, I hope and pray that you make that choice today.

If you're already a Christian, I hope this book ministers to you, too. Living the life you profess isn't as hard as you make it when you realize what it's all about. Actually it's not supposed to be hard at all. You're a Christian because you gave your life to Him. Sometimes we have to give it back to Him and let Him lead the way.

Excuse me for a moment. I'll be right back. I need to pray!

Dear Lord, I pray right now that You use these words from this book to reach people out there. I don't know who this is intended for or who will be reading this. I know that I belong to You and that You will use me for your glory. Please do so today. Thank you Jesus. Amen.

So, here it is folks!

What Does It Mean To Be A
Christian

The Starting Point: Jesus

Christian living begins with having Jesus Christ in your life. Period.

Let me say that again because it's important.

Christian living begins with having Jesus Christ in your life. This means that before you can live the life of a Christian, you have to have Jesus as your Lord and Savior in your life. He has to be the center of your life; the foundation that your life sits on. You can't live a Christian life if you're not a Christian.

No *'buts'* about it!

But, I Go To Church

Going to church does not make you a Christian. It makes you a 'church-goer'. Even though you attend church every Sunday, in the morning and at night, it doesn't make you a Christian. You may be a Sunday school teacher and teach from the Bible. It doesn't make you a Christian.

It's almost like calling yourself a fisherman without a fishing pole. Yes, you may go to the lake, but without a pole, you're just a… person that goes to the lake. You may know everything there is to know about fishing. You may know the different types of fish by the color of their fins and the number of sparkles in their eyes, but it doesn't make you a fisherman. You may have the best fishing boat on the lake, but without the pole, you are basically a boat owner. Are you with me?

But, I Have Christian Family

Just because one of your family members is a Christian doesn't make you one. I know this will be hard for people to believe, but being a Christian is not a genetic thing. It's a Jesus thing!

"My grandfather was a deacon at Flakey Biscuit Baptist Church. He was a Christian man that loved the Lord."

That's great! But, it doesn't make you one. The glitter from your Christian relative's walk doesn't magically fall off on you. It would be nice if it did, but it doesn't. Being a Christian and being saved is about a one on one relationship with Jesus Christ.

But, I Shook The Preacher's Hand Last Sunday

If *'hand shaking'* guaranteed a Christian life, then everybody that visited a church on a Sunday morning would be saved and so would every person that the preacher had come in contact with outside of the church. Think about it! Hand shaking is a greeting, not a magic salvation ticket! That's not how it works!

The Deal?

Here's the deal! A person can only become a Christian when they accept Jesus into their life and get saved. Saved? That's right! The day you realize that you are a sinner and that you are lost without a Savior is the day you have a choice of whether to be a Christian or not. The sad thing is that we are all sinners!

For all have sinned, and come short of the glory of God - Romans 3:23

It's like a day at the lake. You jump in and realize you can't swim! Life was pretty smooth when you were playing close to the bank. But as you drifted out towards the deep part of the water, you realize that you needed a float. The same is true in life. You need to be saved or you will sink like a rock!

"That sounds all fine and dandy, but what am I being saved from?"

The answer is sin. It's those *'bad things'* in your life that goes against God and His way of life. To realize how bad sin is, you must first know who God is.

Who Is God?

God created everything. There is nothing in this world, on Earth, or in outer space that He did not create. He created the water, the air, the trees, animals, and He even created you.

The Bible tells us that He knew us before we were even born and that He knew ALL about us. That tells me He's the one that put us here. He put you here!

Before I formed thee in the belly I knew thee; and before thou camest forth out of the womb I sanctified thee, and I ordained thee a prophet unto the nations. – Jeremiah 1: 5

I believe that we are all here for a purpose - His purpose. But, we will never know this purpose until we give our lives to Him. For a God that created everything in this universe to take the time to make me, tells me I have a purpose for being here. The same is true for you! We need to find out what it is. This will involve getting to know the Creator.

Have you heard this one before?:

For whom he did foreknow, he also did predestinate to be conformed to the image of his Son, that he might be the firstborn among many brethren. – Romans 8: 29

He wants a relationship with you. Since you are here and have a purpose, you will need to get a relationship started with God. You will need to know more about Him. The Bible says God is holy and perfect - sinless. Now keep that thought in your mind for a moment and let's talk again about sin.

When you think of the sin in the world today, what comes to mind? Does murder and stealing? What about lying and foul language? There are all kinds of sin! Small ones to big ones and they all have one thing in common - they are still *'sin'*. Sin is what separates us from a relationship with God. We live in a sinful world and we have sin in our lives. How can we make things right? The unfortunate thing is that WE can't! We need something or someone to fill in that gap. God knew this, too. So what needs to happen?

Don't worry! God already had that planned out because He loves us.

Here's what God did for us! He sent His only Son to die as a sacrifice for our sins. It sounds like a drastic measure to take but it's what was needed. Jesus, His Son, died for us so that we could live - eternally with God.

But wait! His death required something from us?

That's right! It says we have to BELIEVE in Him. Here's another scripture you may have heard:

That if thou shalt confess with thy mouth the Lord Jesus, and shalt believe in thine heart that God hath raised him from the dead, thou shalt be saved. - Romans 10:9

It sounds to me like God has provided a way out for us, but He also requires us to do something to be saved. We already know we are a bunch of sinners. Right?

We are to confess with our mouth the Lord Jesus? And believe in our heart?

Sounds too simple to be true, doesn't it?

It is and it starts with a simple prayer to God. After that, all we have to do is receive this gift of salvation. I believe God convicts our hearts that we are lost. It's like a helpless feeling you have inside that let's you know that you need Him in your life.

Are you feeling that right now? If so, let's get this thing settled. I know a lot of religious people and some Christians get 'weirded out' when you present a model prayer to the lost and ask them to repeat it. I can understand their way of thinking and I know that just repeating prayers doesn't save a person. It has to be heartfelt and sincere. The main points of your prayer has to cover knowing that you're lost without Jesus in your life, understanding that you're a sinner that's sorry for the junk you're doing, and that you are willing to turn from that junk and want Jesus to come in and take over.

That's basically it!

So, if you meet that criteria and would like to accept Jesus as your Lord and Savior, let's do this thing together.

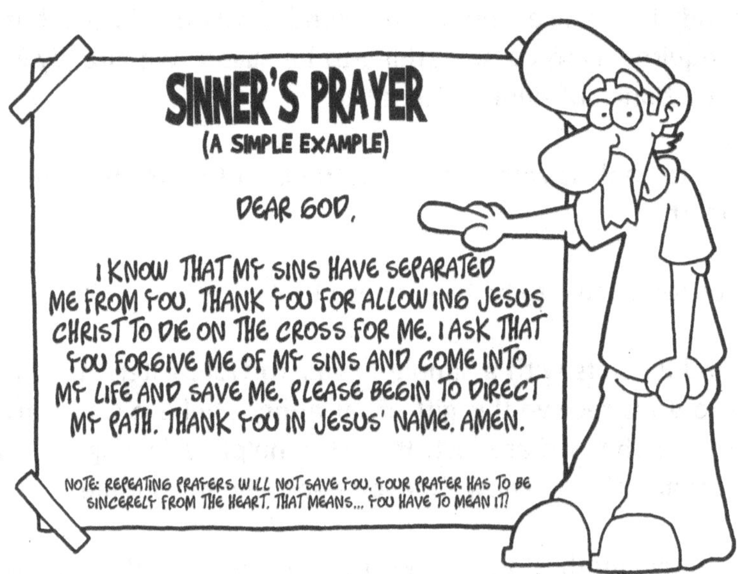

That was easy, wasn't it? Now, I know sparks aren't flying around you and choirs of angels aren't floating by with harps. But, inside you will feel a sense of relief.

It will feel like a ton of bricks have been lifted off your shoulders. Your life may not even show changes immediately, but from this point forward it will. It's like being a new little plant. You will begin growing. That's why they call it being 'born again'. You have a new life! It's up to you make it grow. You can do this by going to church, reading the Bible, and praying every day. Every step in your life from this day on is a 'stepping stone' towards Jesus and growth in your spirituality.

Spiritual Fertilizer

"I'm saved and I know where I'm going when I die. I'm cool with that! But, what should I be doing until then?"

The answer is simple! I should be growing! You should be growing, too! The day we got saved started a new life in us. This is very similar to growing turnip greens in a garden. This new life started as a small seed planted in the ground. Even as a small seed, it's still a turnip green! But you know as well as I do that a plate full of seeds doesn't taste the same as a big plate of turnip greens. The seeds need to grow first.

To help a turnip green grow, it needs some food. Right? It needs some good soil, refreshing water, and some sunlight. The same is true in our Christian walk. Yes, we could stay content with being a seed. But, wouldn't it be better if we started sprouting? A Christian needs some spiritual fertilizer - some

food for the soul.

God provides us with ways to grow. All we have to do is use what He gives us. The soil He provides us is through the relationship we can have in Him through prayer and walking with Him daily. Every day is an opportunity.

We just need to take advantage of it.

Finding a Bible-believing church and actually going to it is a great starting point for growth. I will be the first to admit that going to church was not in my plans. As a young saved *'whooper-snapper'*, I wasn't really a *'people'* person and I hated getting up early on a Sunday morning to hear a long-winded preacher spitting and slobbering on the whole congregation.

The music in church was awful and would always come from people that really shouldn't have been up front singing to people anyway. I spent my time in the back row socializing with my friends. I was young and didn't know what the whole *'church thing'* was about and what it was for.

Church: The Growth Experience

Now that I am older, I realize that it was for my spiritual growth as a baby Christian.

This process of getting up on a Sunday morning, getting dressed, and going to a building and hanging out with all of these *'weird'* people was intended to help me grow. My job was to listen and learn.

I also realize that my attitude towards it was wrong and sitting on the back row was my first mistake. For a young teenager like me, I should have been on the front row listening. Now that I look back, maybe my life wouldn't have drifted away from God as it did. I'll explain more on this later on in this book.

What is *'going to church'* all about?

A church building is a place where believers gather to worship and praise God. It's just a building and as I explained earlier, by *'just*

going' doesn't save you. Only God can do that! We go there to worship Him and praise Him for who He is – He's God!

It's also a place to *'get your learning on'*. This is accomplished by singing praises, praying, and listening to what the preacher has to say. God uses these tools to teach us stuff from His Word.

O come, let us sing unto the LORD: let us make a joyful noise to the rock of our salvation. – Psalm 95: 1

Depending on the church, the music is a big part of worship. There are many scriptures throughout the Bible that encourages us to sing songs of praises to God. Actually, the Book of Psalms is simply a book full of song lyrics. It can be in a traditional music style or contemporary music style. It really doesn't matter as long as it's joyful. People will argue about the type of music being played at church and say that only one style is acceptable, but it's not about the style as it is the *'heart'* in which it's worshiped. No one ever taught me this concept about Christian music, but it was in the Bible if I had just taken the time to read it. Plus, when you are singing with right heart, the bad singers start to sound pretty good. Our focus is more on what they are singing instead of how well they sing it. And that's the truth!

A preacher plays a big part in the service because he is a God-called man to deliver the Word. He is the guy that stands in the front of the church with the suit on. If you are in a Baptist church, you will recognize him because he will be the one that speaks the loudest and has the biggest belly. He will be the sweaty man that spits on the congregation sitting on the front row during the services. He is also the first one in line at the *'all you can eat'* buffet dinner restaurant after the church services are over. I'm sorry. I had to throw that in there.

Being a preacher is a big responsibility. The Lord gives him a message to share with the people at church. It is up to him to deliver it. If he delivers something that was not given to him by God, he is going to be in some serious trouble. The preacher has to be very careful in his preaching. He is responsible for what comes out of his mouth.

Preachers ain't perfect! They're human just like we are!

On the flip side of this, we have to realize that the preacher is just a man. He will make mistakes and is not perfect. Many people will stop going to a particular church or to church, in general, because of something a preacher did that was not acceptable. We should not be followers of preachers, but followers of Jesus Christ. However, we should listen as the Word is being presented to us and follow along with our Bibles open. Listening was another mistake I made earlier in my life.

Prayer: For More Growth

Praying is our way of communicating with God. Just like with all types of relationships, good communication is the way to make it stronger. That's why a lot of marriages don't work

out. Many times it's because one person does all the talking, or no one is listening, or that nobody talks or listens at all. It just doesn't work!

Prayer keeps our spiritual life alive! Don't you want to live? Get your prayer on!

By praying to God, we can ask for forgiveness of our sins. We can tell Him how our day is going and let Him know the areas we need help. We can ask for things in our life and even pray for other people's needs. It's like talking to a good friend or better yet, we are talking directly to our Father in Heaven. It helps us to grow spiritually, especially when we see the things we pray for come to pass.

Praying is done in church. It can be done as a group or you can pray as an individual at the altar or right where you sit. But, it's not the only place! You can pray anytime and anywhere. You can pray at home, at somebody else's home, or even on aisle 3 at your local Wally World. It doesn't matter as long as you pray! Most importantly, pray daily!

Bible: The Growth Continues

There's a book that sits around in many homes all over the world.

It's usually the one that's tucked away with dust covering it. It's called the Bible. Even though many people own it, it's rare that people actually read it! For a Christian, it's like an instruction manual for living. It's food for the soul. Its God's words in book form so that we can grow spiritually.

The problem is that many people see it is as just a book with words; like a hard to read novel. It's full of 'thee's' and 'thou's' and it's hard to understand. It has stories in there that really don't apply to us, right? Wrong!

Living the Christian life requires reading the instruction manual.

Have you ever tried to put something together or use something

without the manual? There were always parts left over or it didn't work the way it's supposed to. Right?

The same is true in our Christian walk. If you try it without the manual, you'll end up face down in the middle of the road. I know from experience, but I am thankful that Jesus was there to pick me up!

There is so much stuff written in the pages of the Bible. It covers everything! Any topic you want to know about, it's in there! There's anything from basic life principles to the history of man. It does include stories of people and their experiences. Why? The purpose is so that we can use their life of accomplishments or mistakes to help make ours better. We can learn from them. It's so cool! The more you put into it, the more you will get out of it.

To sum it all up, basic spiritual growth begins with going to church, prayer and reading the Bible. You can only grow from here!

The Battle Is On! Like A Chicken Bone

Just when you thought that being a Christian was easy, bad things come into your life. Troubles seem to come at you like darts flying at you from everywhere. It may seem like you are now being tempted with things from your past. You may be tempted with things that affect your weaknesses. It's all part of the plan.

It's a battle and we have an enemy! Satan is his name. You may have heard of him. Don't be '*skeered*'! He's not that cute little cartoon you see on television and he's not that scary demon you see in the horror movies. According to the Bible, he is an angel – a fallen angel. He was with God before the world began. He has been trying to mess things up from the day that God created Adam and Eve.

Remember hearing about Adam and Eve?

In the first few chapters of Genesis, you'll read where Satan tempted them into eating the forbidden fruit. By doing so, sin began and it has been growing ever since. He is in the world today along with

his band of devils trying to trip people up. He tries to prevent people from getting saved and makes life hard for the average Christian. The purpose in all of this is to mess up God's work in this world and in His work in the people that live in it.

Keep this in mind, God is creating and preparing a place for His people. Folks, this world that we currently live in is not our home! He is returning one day to take his people to their real home. Who gets to go? It's the people that have been saved. That is why Satan works so hard. His days are numbered and he already knows where he's going and it's not good. His purpose is to take people with him - the lost and unsaved. Did you get that?

I bet you're thinking...

I'm saved, so why is he messing with me?

That's an easy question to answer. You could be the link to someone else getting saved. Your witness and testimony could be what leads them to a relationship with the Lord. You will notice that he works on you the hardest when you are trying to live right. If you are living sinfully, Satan doesn't have to do much to you. You have already lost your witnessing ability. What else does he need to do? He's got you right where he wants you - **DEFEATED**.

But, as you grow in the Lord, you are gaining strength and will be used to reach others. Satan hates this idea and will start throwing the darts. He wants you dead and out of the picture! You have become a hindrance to his master minded plans. Watch out!

That's why it is so important to apply

the *'spiritual fertilizer'* to your life - church, prayer, and Bible. When you are following Jesus, you will be able to recognize Satan's devilish schemes against you.

There hath no temptation taken you but such as is common to man: but God is faithful, who will not suffer you to be tempted above that ye are able; but will with the temptation also make a way to escape, that ye may be able to bear it. – 1 Corinthians 10: 13

Here's where it gets tricky. As a child of God, He is watching over you. There is nothing that Satan does to you that God doesn't know about. As mean as it may sound, God allows Satan to tempt you. Yep! That's right! We can learn this from the Book of Job. This doesn't make God bad! It is part of His way of strengthening you as a Christian.

However, He will never let you be tempted more than you can bear without His help!

Temptations are coming. What are they? These will be the things that come into your life that make you think,

"Hmm...Should I or shouldn't I?"

This could be almost anything. Temptations come from Satan and are directed by God. As we discussed earlier, temptations will either make us stronger or they will defeat us if we agree to give in to them.

You can almost know what your temptations will be by knowing what your weaknesses are. If the Lord rescued you from abusing drugs and alcohol, you can be guaranteed that these will come back into your life in the form of a temptation. The temptation in itself is not wrong, it's when you give into them that it becomes a sin. Are you hearing me?

Many people suffer from spiritual depression because they don't know why they are being tempted with these things that may have destroyed them in the past. They think it's their fault and feel like they have been defeated. Here's your wake up call! It's just a

temptation! That's all! Rebuke it and send it back to Satan from where it came! Keep moving on and get over it! Don't let it get you down! If you're down and out because of it, then Satan has won the battle anyway.

Submit yourselves therefore to God. Resist the devil, and he will flee from you. – James 4: 7

Once again, temptations come from Satan. Always remember that! It's important to know.

Trials, on the other hand, are a different story. What are trials? I'll try to explain. Trials, sometimes called *'valleys'*, enter our lives from time to time. They usually appear when things seem to be going great.

They can almost be like a messed up deer hunting trip. You deer hunters will be able to relate to this. You are wearing your camouflage sitting up in a deer stand. Everything is going great! You have your gun ready and deer are everywhere! It's going to be a great hunting day! All of a sudden it starts to rain! The deer scatter and you have to climb down from the tree soaking wet. Your legs start chaffing as you walk the long trail back to our 4 x 4 pick up truck. You are feeling miserable and you weren't able to get a deer.

Why did this have to happen? Why do you have to go through this?

You call your friend, Bob, on your outdated cell phone telling him what you just went through as you drive back home disgusted with the way the day ended. You are going through all kinds of emotions. You are mad, sad and everything else other than glad. You know what I'm saying?

The next day, you try hunting again. Before you leave, you check the weather report on the news to see if it will rain. The weatherman says, *"It will be sunny all day!"* You bring an umbrella and an extra pair of socks anyway – just in case. This time you pull your trailer carrying your ATV (All Terrain Vehicle) that you got for Christmas last year with you in case of an emergency. Now you are prepared and learned a lesson!

The purpose of this long drawn out story is to say that God is ultimately in control and allows trials to happen in your life to make you stronger. There is something about them that help you develop character. They make you better prepared for future

trials and you are able to use the experience to teach others and help them. Remember Bob from the story? Guess what? He doesn't go deer hunting anymore without bringing an extra pair of socks because he learned something from your experience, too. Pretty cool, huh?

Just like temptations, trials seem to focus on your weak areas in your walk with Jesus.

Suppose you have a love for money and material things. Guess what your trial will be? Yep, you guessed it! Money issues! It could happen in the form of losing your job or down time in your business. Who knows? But, the important things you will learn from it are to trust God with all of your heart, He is your provider – NOT YOU, and to be content with what you have. I know this one from personal experience.

What if you have anger issues? Guess what your trial will be? You will be hit with things in order to make you mad. You will eventually learn to control your temper and thank God for working with you.

The victories come when we *pass the tests'*. When you are tempted and you are able to push it away, you have just won a victory. Congratulations!

When you are in a trial and you make it through praising God, you have just won a victory. You are on a roll! Now take a look at yourself. You are stronger, better, and more usable to God to win others to Him. It's all part of the process and you're in it! Why would God go through all of this trouble for you?

That's an easy one. He loves you!

The final victory comes when Jesus returns to take us home to be with Him. What an awesome day that will be! Now that you know the basics of being a Christian and what it's all about, it's time to *'walk the walk'*. This means *'being a light in the world'* and sharing what you know about Jesus. I would be lying to you if I said it was easy. It's not! The temptations and the fact that we are all just too lazy prevent us from doing everything the Lord requires us to do.

Walkin' the Walk

There are a lot of people out there that will say that they are a Christian. It's not up to us to decide if they are speaking the truth. This is up to them and their relationship with God. But, I believe if we are going to say we are a Christian, we need to show it in the way we live our lives. We need to *'walk the walk'*.

As a child of God, our life should show a change. That means we shouldn't be doing the old sinful things we used to do. This life should reflect Jesus. Have you heard the old saying, *"What would Jesus*

do?"? This question could be applied to every choice we have to make.

I also know that we aren't perfect. We are going to make mistakes. But, we shouldn't let that way of thinking prevent us from trying. We should strive to be like Jesus every day.

Here's an example:

What if the tire company, **Not Good Enough Year**, thought the same way. What if they thought, "Well, I know I'm supposed to make good tires and that people out there depend on me to provide them, but I'm not perfect. So, I'll just sit here and sorta throw something together and see what happens."

I imagine a lot of people driving cars and trucks will be affected by it. Some will end up in ditches and may never get to their destination. You see where I'm going with this? It's about making the effort to do the best you can. People's lives are at stake!

'Off' With The Old
And 'On' With The New

Before you were saved, you may have been in a lifestyle that you know Jesus wouldn't approve of. This could be almost anything. I won't sit here and list the many things that could fall in this category because you know the ones that pertain to you. These made up the 'old' self of your sinful nature.

Now, here's the problem. You are saved and still doing the *'old'* things that you used to do. Your *'new'* life doesn't reflect a change. You are not living by what you read in the Bible or what you are being taught at church, but by your sinful nature. It could be that you are not reading the Bible or going to church at all and are just *'winging'* your new Christian walk. It's not going to work!

This creates a bad situation in your relationship with

Jesus and to others around you. You are missing out on the spiritual joy of being saved. You are basically the 'old' you with a Jesus label. This is good if all you want is a free ticket to Eternity. But that's not what being a Christian is about. God has a purpose for you and will use you, if you let Him, to reach out to others. That's when *'being saved'* gets exciting and has a greater meaning in your life. Allow Him to change you!

The Suit And Tie Christian

Before I start on this topic, let me tell you that wearing a suit and tie is not a bad thing. Actually, Christians that wear suits and ties look good and I mean that. That is the main purpose of saying it: Christians that just *'look'* good. A person could be sinfully rotten to the core, but when they put a suit and tie on, they fit in with the rest of the Christians in church on Sunday morning.

Being a Christian is a spiritual thing - it's what's on the inside that counts. It's a relationship with Jesus Christ that goes straight to the heart. When this kind of relationship goes to the heart, it will begin to manifest itself outwards in our actions and in our words. Are you with me?

Many people are deceived by the *'suit and tie'* Christian because they only *'look'* good. If you were to spend some time with them, you would realize what is really going on in their heart. You could see it in their actions in the way they conduct their life. When they speak, their words coming out would make you think differently of them.

Knowing that, it is important to realize that *'walking the walk'* is more than just trying to look good. It's about *'looking good'* because of the relationship we have in Jesus and what He has placed in our heart.

Holier Than Thou Christian

I have met some Christian people that are quick to judge people. Being a Christian myself, these people were quick to tell me everything that I was doing wrong. This made me want to quit going to church and socializing with the *'Christian'* people. I later learned that this type of judging is OK when you are trying to help someone and are doing it in a loving way. This should also be followed by a solution to their problem.

Pride is a killer, folks! People can easily fill themselves with the pride of being a Christian and the spiritual things they know that not only do they kill their witnessing abilities but they actually kill the chances of bringing others to Jesus. They can also kill the growth of other Christians. It's a bad deal! Jesus wasn't about all that!

If you read the Bible and learn how Jesus

was, you'll learn that He never had this type of attitude toward others. He had compassion for His followers in teaching them how they should and shouldn't be and He had compassion for the ones that didn't know Him. By His example is why people chose to follow Him. He would socialize with the sinners and lead them by being the example. He didn't walk around with a stick bopping people on the hands every time they did something wrong. If He did see something wrong in a person's life, He would lovingly tell them and provide a solution. This is how we should be.

It's great to be a Christian and to have grown spiritually in our walk. But we need to understand that without God's mercy on our life and His spiritual guidance, we are nothing more than a sinner ourselves. When we meet people that are lost, we need to focus on the sin in their lives and not on that person.

And remember God loves them, too.

It's Not Just About Us
It's About Others

The day we became saved, God could have just taken us home to be with Him. We're saved! What other reason would we need to be here on Earth? Since we don't belong here anymore, we may as well just move on to Glory Land. So, why are we still here?

Listen to this:

Go ye therefore, and teach all nations, baptizing them in the name of the Father, and of the Son, and of the Holy Ghost: Teaching them to observe all things whatsoever I have commanded you: and, lo, I am with you alway, even unto the end of the world. Amen. – Matthew 28: 19, 20

Jesus said it right there. We are called to be His disciples to go out and teach others. A disciple is a follower of Jesus; to follow

His teachings and to be like Him. Just like the twelve disciples in the Bible, we have a mission statement:

"To be a light in the world and to lead others to Jesus by spreading the Gospel and being an example to the world."

Being a Christian means being Christ-like. You may not know this, but being a Christian is not just about you. The world teaches us to be concerned about ourselves and nobody else. What do we want out of life? How can we make our life better? Watch television and you will discover that all of the commercial ads are directed to you.

This is not what Jesus is all about. Your Christian life should reflect the One that saved you. Why is this so important?

Here's the scenario:

- **The world is full of people that don't know Jesus as their Lord and Savior.**
- **Jesus is returning one day to take His children home.**
- **The ones that remain will burn in a lake of fire.**

Who are His children? It's the people that are saved. Does He want everyone to spend Eternity with Him? Yes, He does.

Unfortunately, it's this thing called 'sin' that we talked about a few pages back that separates us. He gives us all a *'freedom of choice'.* It's a choice to turn from sin, ask for forgiveness and to turn to Him. It's plain and simple! We have a choice!

What is our role as a Christian in all of this? The answer is to lead others to Him. It's about *'being a light in the world'.* We are the link that connects them to a relationship with Jesus. We can't save them, but we can lead them to the One that can. Is this sinking in?

This is why it's so important to truly *'walk the walk'.* It's not so that WE can live a better life, but to show others the *'better life'* we have in Jesus. Think about it!

When you start living the life Jesus wants you to have, people are going to want it, too. If they don't see a change in you, then how will they know Jesus? Time is running short! What are you waiting on? Walk the walk! Be a light!

My Testimony

A testimony is what you have after the Lord saves you or delivers you from something. It's like our story to tell others of what Jesus has done for us. Every Christian will have one. If you are saved today, you have one, too.

Our testimony is what we will use to lead others to Jesus. It is how we are able to witness to other

people. Believe it or not, that *'thing'* that Jesus delivered you from is probably what is holding a lot of people you meet back from a relationship with Jesus. It is very interesting how this works. It's like God will put people that are not saved in your life that will need to hear your testimony. The amazing thing is that they are going through the same thing or have been through it and don't know how to deal with it. All of a sudden they meet you; a person with a similar story, but this time there is a solution. His name is Jesus.

I accepted Jesus as my Lord and Savior when I was 14 years old. My father had left me and my mother when I was five and she was forced to raise me on her own. The Lord stepped in during my teenage years because I needed a father in my life. He became my Heavenly Father!

Do you realize what happens to many teenagers growing up without a father? Let's just say that many of them end up going down the wrong roads in life. They wind up in places and situations that they shouldn't be in. God gave me His protection and put me on the path of righteousness as long as I stayed focused in it.

Within that same year, I also met Satan. I didn't really recognize him at first because he disguised himself in the things I allowed in my life. Pornography was his first trick. This is a big temptation for a young kid with raging hormones, but I took the bait. This went on for years and found its way on my computer screen as I got older.

Satan also knew I had a passion for music. I enjoyed listening to it and playing it on the guitar. Its original purpose was intended to glorify and praise God, but wound up on the stages at the local bars playing as a live band.

This introduced a new temptation given by Satan that created an addiction within me that I would later battle with in life. It's the poison called alcohol. It destroys you from the inside out and affects the people around you. Alcohol every day pushes the family away! And that's exactly what it was doing. Because of my addiction, I would be re-creating my life story all over again with my kids. They would be fatherless and the vicious cycle would continue.

That's when Jesus showed up! He woke me up when my son got saved. At that time, my son needed someone to lead him to the Lord and I wasn't able to do it. I should have been, but couldn't. My life was a mess! I had to take him to someone that could. This burned me deep and helped me realize that I needed Jesus back in my life, too. It wasn't that I need to be saved again. It was that I needed to go back to where I left Him. I had turned away.

Years later, the pornography is gone and the alcohol has been traded in for the living water that Jesus freely offers. I have been *'living'* since then. This new change has created a great life for me and my family. It has created a ministry that God has used has to reach many people and touch lives. I realize now that this was part of God's original plan before I decided to change it. I am ashamed that it took twenty years to wake me up. This is my testimony. Thank you Jesus!

Once again, the main purpose of this book is to use what the Lord has given me to share with you.

My heart goes out to all Christians everywhere – all over the world. If the lessons I have learned from my life can be used to help someone out there, then that's what I want to do. I'm sure there are Christian people out there like me that don't know what the whole deal is. Some are blinded by Satan on their purpose on this Earth and what they should be doing until the Lord comes back. I hope this book will prevent them from wasting 20 years of their life going in the wrong direction.

If you don't know Jesus as your Lord and Savior, I encourage you to make that step. Being a Christian isn't what the world says it is. It's being what Jesus wants us to be: happy and full of joy. If you need that in your life today, Jesus can and will freely give it to you. All you have to do is ask Him.

If you're a Christian, begin living by His Word and reading it daily. Don't sit around like stagnated water! Do something with the new life God has given you. Reach out to people that need this life, too. Learn more about Jesus. Live the life that He wants you to live. It brings life – life abundantly. Let's do something! You know?

I hope you received what you needed today. And please share this book with someone you know!

More From A BackPew Review

Thanks for reading this guide. We hope you enjoyed it and will continue to read our other guides in the series. Here is a complete list of our books from the series:

- **What Does It Mean To Be A Christian**
- **Acts: The Early Days Of The Christian Church**
- **Being A Dad According To The Bible**
- **The Prison Letters: Apostle Paul's Letters To The Early Church**
- **Exodus: The Journey To The Promised Land**
- **Genesis: The Beginning, The Fall And The Promise**
- **The Seven Letters: The New Testament Letters To The Early Church**
- **The Gospel From A Four-Sided View**
- **Healthy Eating: A Few Tips From The Bible**
- **Being A Man According To The Bible**
- **A Marriage Built To Last: Learn What The Bible Says About Marriage**
- **How Do I Pray? The Bible Tells Us How**
- **Revelation: The End Is Near?**